the DIRECTOR'S HANDBOOK

Pinsent Masons LLP

Pinsent Masons is an international law firm delivering solutions that enable its clients to meet their commercial objectives. With over 270 partners and a total legal team of 1,000 lawyers worldwide, we can offer full support to growing businesses and established corporates.

A fundamental commitment to delivering good client service has led the firm to invest in building strength in all the areas of law that are key to business. This expertise is overlaid with significant experience in a number of market sectors, providing it with a more immediate understanding of the regulatory burdens and liabilities faced by those operating in different industries.

It is Pinsent Masons' depth of knowledge of these sectors and strength of commitment to them, both in the United Kingdom and overseas, that distinguishes the firm, enabling it to give advice that is appropriate to both sector and circumstances.

For more information call 0845 300 32 32 or visit www.pinsentmasons.com

Institute of Directors

The IoD supports, represents and sets standards for directors. It is a non-party-political business organisation founded in 1903 and granted its Royal Charter in 1906.

Membership includes leaders from the complete spectrum of business – from media to manufacturing, e-business to the public sector. Members include CEOs of large corporations as well as entrepreneurial directors of start-up companies. They are represented in 92 per cent of FTSE 100 companies, but 70 per cent are directors of small and medium-sized enterprises.

The IoD offers a wide range of business services including business centre facilities across the United Kingdom and on the Continent, conferences, networking events, publications and information services. It provides authoritative representation of the interests of business to government and policymakers, enabling business leaders' views to be influential in the development of public policy.

A key objective of the IoD is to promote professionalism in the boardroom. It has established a certified qualification for directors – Chartered Director – and runs specific board- and director-level training and individual career mentoring programmes.

For more information call 020 7766 8888 or visit www.iod.com.

the DIRECTOR'S HANDBOOK

Your duties, responsibilities and liabilities

EDITED BY

MARTIN WEBSTER

RECOMMENDED BY
INSTITUTE OF DIRECTORS

Pinsent Masons

KoganPage

LONDON PHILADELPHIA NEW DELHI

This book has been published by the Institute of Directors in association with Pinsent Masons, and in association with Kogan Page.

The views expressed in this book are those of the authors and are not necessarily the same as those of the Institute of Directors.

Information in this book is correct at the time of writing, 1 February 2010.

Publisher's note
Every possible effort has been made to ensure that the information contained in this book is accurate at the time of going to press, and the publishers and authors cannot accept responsibility for any errors or omissions, however caused. No responsibility for loss or damage occasioned to any person acting, or refraining from action, as a result of the material in this publication can be accepted by the editor, the publisher or any of the authors. Readers should consult their advisers before acting on any issues raised.

First published in Great Britain in 2005 by the Institute of Directors
Second edition 2007
Third edition 2010
Reprinted 2014 (twice), 2015 (three times)

2nd Floor, 45 Gee Street
London EC1V 3RS
United Kingdom
www.koganpage.com

ISBN 978 0 7494 6058 7

British Library Cataloguing-in-Publication Data

A CIP record for this book is available from the British Library.

Typeset by Jean Cussons Typesetting Ltd, Diss, Norfolk
Printed and bound by CPI Group (UK) Ltd, Croydon, CR0 4YY

Contents

Acknowledgements

In compiling the third edition of this book, I have had the help of several expert authors. Chapters that have been written by my colleagues at Pinsent Masons include:

- Service contracts – Robert Mecrate-Butcher

- Remuneration issues – Rory Cray

- Pensions – Nicola Bumpus and Alastair Meeks

- Health and safety and corporate manslaughter – Kevin Bridges

- Financial difficulty and insolvency – Jonathan Jeffries and Dawn Allen

I am grateful for other valuable material from Alan Davis, Tim Dolan, Liz Morgan and Kizzy Augustin and indeed for the help and support of all my partners and colleagues at the firm.

Tom Nash's enthusiasm for the project has been an enormous encouragement throughout and his wise counsel and gentle handling of a sometimes stressed author have proved a great help. Caroline Proud's formidable sub-editing skills and willingness to challenge our first thoughts once again brought a welcome clarity and brevity to both our thinking and the text.

Martin Webster
Pinsent Masons LLP
London, February 2010

Important Resource in a Changing World

The credit crunch has placed an even stronger spotlight on the role of boards. Questions have been raised about how they function and about the regulatory framework surrounding them.

The Financial Reporting Council's consultation on the Combined Code showed strong and widespread support for the view that the UK governance model works and that the 'comply or explain' regime is the right approach. At the same time, however, it highlighted the belief that weaknesses in the performance of some boards played a part in the financial crisis and that more active and professional governance needs to be the standard for the future.

Due diligence, induction and evaluation by, for and of directors have therefore increased in importance and seriousness. Directors should be fully aware of their responsibilities and they should be confident in discharging them. This handbook will help on both counts.

The environment directors operate in continues to be dynamic.

Some modest changes in the Code are intended to increase transparency and accountability to shareholders, while discussions on a Stewardship Code are intended to place a parallel emphasis on engagement by investors with boards. For banks, the Financial Services Authority is also taking a more active approach to the authorisation of board members, and imposing further sector-specific governance requirements, notably the creation of a risk committee in addition to, and distinct from, the audit committee. But on all boards, committee work is becoming more important and demanding. Many major companies are creating new committees to focus on environmental; social responsibility; health and safety issues, while audit work is increasing.

The challenges facing remuneration committees are also becoming greater. The credit crunch exposed some misalignment between executives and shareholders in the design of remuneration schemes, and caused more questions to be asked about the size of executive pay packages, particularly but not exclusively in the financial sector. At the same time, however, the pressure for multiple performance criteria in remuneration schemes has increased complexity to the point where incentives are often obscured or blunted. Institutional investors are voting more actively on remuneration issues, and are urging more frequent election of some or all directors to give them the opportunity to express their discontent.

Shareholders expect boards to identify and manage risk, set the risk tolerance level for the company, explain the 'business model' and, increasingly, also be aware of their wider social responsibilities. With all these requirements go expectations that they can produce annual reports that are clear and concise yet comprehensive.

Meanwhile, the development of accounting standards poses its own challenges for directors, and the framework of law puts them at risk on a wide range of issues, not least anti-competitive behaviour.

With all these demands, it may seem surprising that people are still willing to take on the role of non-executive director. Clearly, some are thinking very hard before agreeing to join a board. And so they should. But with proper preparation, and continuing attention, the role of the director is still a fascinating one – and involvement in either the creation of a successful business or the turnaround of an unsuccessful one can give great personal satisfaction.

I have now sat on a wide range of corporate boards and can give personal testimony to this.

I hope this handbook will help you to enjoy your role, too!

Sarah Hogg
Chairman, Financial Reporting Council

Manual for the Modern Director

The vast majority of directors know that for their businesses to succeed they need to combine entrepreneurialism and risk taking with professionalism and expertise. That means complying with the law and following best practice.

Company law is a central component of the overall UK business environment. Directors can only maximise their contribution to the performance of their enterprises if they are aware of its key features. However, the difficulty for many people in business is finding accessible sources of information and support.

Fulfilling these informational needs is a key part of the IoD's mission. The IoD exists to support, represent and set standards for UK directors. We represent the interests of directors to government and others, and seek to promote a regulatory regime that encourages (rather than impedes) well-run businesses.

We are the premier provider of training and development for directors: our Chartered Director qualification, the world's first accredited qualification for directors, is increasingly recognised as the hallmark of a competent and highly professional director.

We want to raise the standards of directorship but, at the same time, we know how complex the task can be. We know that the burden of regulation is one of the main concerns of our members, most of whom run SMEs without the benefit of specialist in-house teams to guide them through the potential minefields. Directors frequently feel very much alone. Even when government sets out to simplify the rules, the sheer volume of regulation can seem overwhelming.

Directors cannot plead ignorance of the law as it affects them and their companies. But few of them can reasonably be expected to be legal experts; changes in the law can easily catch them out.

To help fill the information gap and provide practical support for those running businesses, we publish *The Director's Handbook*. Since the first edition came out in 2005, there has been a major reform of UK company law in the shape of the Companies Act 2006 – at exactly 1,300 sections, reputedly the largest single piece of legislation ever.

The Act, which was introduced in stages between 2006 and 2009, affects all companies, large and small. While much of the law has not changed in substance, there are important new provisions such as the statutory statement of directors' duties, rules on derivative actions and significant changes in the regime for private companies.

A competent director needs to be able to judge when it is appropriate to seek professional help – and to know how to apply any advice that is provided. This latest edition of the handbook guides directors through some of the complexities of the 2006 Act. Like its predecessors, it is an invaluable source of information and advice across a wide range of issues. We are again delighted with the efforts of Martin Webster and the team at Pinsent Masons, who have succeeded in producing a guide to law and good practice that is both authoritative and accessible.

This is not intended to be a legal textbook, but a work for directors to use in their business lives. It draws on real examples, with which many directors will be familiar, to make its points.

Although this book is primarily aimed at directors of companies incorporated under the Companies Acts, much of the subject matter is also of relevance to many other types of organisation – be they in the private, public or voluntary sectors. Board-level skills are applicable in a wide range of contexts, and it is encouraging that directors are serving in an increasingly diverse range of organisations at differing stages of their careers.

I hope that you will find this book as useful and informative as I have – I commend it to you.

Miles Templeman
Director General
Institute of Directors

Preface

This book is designed to be a practical guide for all those who are directors of companies or perform an equivalent role. It is neither a legal textbook nor an exhaustive statement of the law as it applies to directors; rather, it aims to be an accessible source of advice and best practice for people who face real issues in their daily working lives.

In planning this book, we wanted to cover a number of specific areas where directors commonly encounter risk in fulfilling their responsibilities. All of the authors are practising lawyers who each day advise directors of their rights and liabilities and help them in finding practical answers to problems. We hope the chapters that follow are a distillation of that advice and help and will be a real resource for those who run companies and need to understand the ever-changing legal and regulatory environment in which they operate.

Except as specifically mentioned, the law is stated as at 1 February, 2010.

Martin Webster
Pinsent Masons LLP
London, February 2010

Introduction

1. Basic principles of company law

Companies come in many different shapes and sizes; there are key differences in what they can and cannot do, and the purpose for which each is designed. But all are separate legal persons independent of their directors and shareholders. Only rarely will the law look behind a company and treat it as being the same person as those who control it.

This concept of a company as a separate legal personality has two consequences:

■ A company's property belongs to it and not to its directors, management or shareholders. Even if you are a sole director and a 100 per cent shareholder, you can still be found guilty of stealing from your own company. Liquidators and future owners will have an interest in pursuing claims for theft or misuse of assets where a company has been plundered by those in day-to-day control. Many a corporate swindler has been pursued through the courts for forgetting this basic principle.

■ A company is responsible for its own debts and liabilities. The shareholders and, as a general rule, directors cannot be forced to pay them.

That second point is why 'limited' companies give their shareholders 'limited liability'. A limited company may be sued until all its assets have been exhausted, but no creditor can turn to the shareholders and ask them to meet any deficit. Once a company has received at least the nominal value of its issued shares (£1 for a £1 share, etc), the shares are 'fully paid' and the shareholder has no further liability. Shares may be issued 'partly paid': a £1 share may be issued with 25p payable on issue and 75p at some future date or on an earlier liquidation. But once those amounts are paid in full, the shareholder has no further liability for the company's debts.

These basic principles underlie much of what follows in this book. But it is important to remember they are principles of company law. In the field of tax in particular, many inroads have been made by both statute and the courts that allow the authorities to look behind company structures at who really owns and controls the entity.

Most companies are 'limited by shares', and they may be 'private' or 'public' companies. Public companies may have their shares 'listed' or traded on a stock exchange – although they are under no obligation to do so.

If a company is not limited by shares, it may be 'limited by guarantee', or it may be unlimited. All of these different types of company are explained below.

2. Different types of company

Private limited company

All companies that are not public companies are defined by law as private. Being a private company is the default position. Private companies can range from a small family company to a subsidiary in a large group that is a substantial trading entity in its own right. Sometimes, they will simply be trading vehicles for one or two individuals who want the benefit of limited liability or the added kudos of trading as a company.

As such, the private company is a very flexible format that can be adapted to fit numerous different requirements. But the one thing that a private company cannot do as a matter of law is offer its shares to the public. Any private company that wants to issue shares to the public must first become a plc or public limited company.

Private companies will, therefore, usually have fewer shareholders than a public company, and there will often be restrictions on the transfer of their shares. Those with a very small number of shareholders, including those that are subsidiaries, might ban all transfers of shares that are not first approved by the board of directors. This allows the board to control who becomes a shareholder and, ultimately, who controls the company.

Companies with a larger shareholder base might have more sophisticated rules that allow the transfer of shares by a shareholder but first require that they are offered to existing shareholders (under 'pre-emption provisions'), thereby giving them the opportunity to keep ownership within the existing group and to exclude new shareholders.

Public limited company

If you want to be a public rather than a private company, you must take a number of steps. You will need:

■ A name that ends with the words 'public limited company' (or the Welsh equivalent); permitted abbreviations are PLC, plc or Plc.

■ An issued share capital with a nominal value of at least £50,000 and paid up share capital of at least £12,500 (or the equivalent in euros). You could, for example, issue 50,000 £1 shares, or 250,000 20p shares, each paid up at least to one quarter of its nominal value – 50,000 £1 shares paid up as to 25p on each share, or 250,000 20p shares paid up as to 5p on each. (There is no equivalent minimum for a private company.)

A public company is subject to more stringent controls than a private one in a number of areas. Some of them are listed below.

■ The rules on making loans to directors are more restrictive for all companies in a group where one of the members is a public company (see section 7 in Chapter 2).

■ A public company can purchase or redeem its own shares, but it can only pay for them by using those profits from which dividends can be paid. A private company, on the other hand, has the option of using its capital if distributable profits fall short.

■ It is a criminal offence for a public company to give financial assistance for the purchase of its own shares, for example by lending money to someone buying a stake in the company. Since October 2008, there has been no equivalent ban for private companies.

■ Many private companies are allowed to prepare abbreviated accounts each year. Public companies, on the other hand, have to prepare and file with Companies House a full set of accounts, and pay the added costs that may involve.

■ A public company must have a company secretary and hold an AGM each year; a private company can dispense with both.

Listed companies

A public company may have its shares admitted to the Official List of the UK Listing Authority (part of the Financial Services Authority), with its shares traded on the London Stock Exchange. It will then be said to be a 'listed' company. One may also talk about a company's shares being 'quoted' or traded on other markets in London – including the Alternative Investment Market (AIM) and PLUS – or anywhere else in the world.

Having your shares traded on a public market will inevitably bring increased obligations for directors – be they statutory or regulatory. Many of these obligations are explained in the later chapters of this book.

Holding companies and subsidiaries

If company A owns more than 50 per cent of the issued shares of company B, it is clear that A is B's holding company and B is therefore a subsidiary of A. But the definition of 'subsidiary' and 'holding company' in the Companies Act goes beyond that simple example and covers a number of other situations. B will be a subsidiary of A if:

■ A holds a majority of voting rights in B: it's voting rights, not just shares, that are important.

■ A is a shareholder of B and has the right to appoint or remove a majority of the directors.

■ A is a shareholder of B and controls a majority of the voting rights in B as a result of an agreement it has with other shareholders.

Other key points include:

■ If C is a subsidiary of B, it also counts as a subsidiary of A.

■ B will be a 'wholly owned subsidiary' of A if its only shareholders are A and A's other subsidiaries or nominees acting on A's behalf.

■ Shares held in B on behalf of A are treated as being held by A.

■ Shares held in a trust for others do not count: if B holds shares in A as trustee of, say, A's pension fund, it will not be treated as owning shares in A. (Generally, a subsidiary cannot hold shares in its own holding company.)

A company with more than one trading activity has the choice of carrying on all its trades under the umbrella of one company or splitting them between a number of trading subsidiaries. Its decision will probably depend on the factors below.

- **Risk mitigation** – having a number of companies in the group, each with the benefits of limited liability, can be an advantage. If one subsidiary gets into financial difficulties there is nothing in law that obliges its parent to continue supporting it, unless it has guaranteed the subsidiary's liabilities or otherwise agreed to help.

- **Tax** – as a general rule, whatever trading structure is used, the effect should be tax neutral, but there are numerous examples where some advantage, or disadvantage, can arise from keeping separate activities in separate subsidiaries or, conversely, from lumping them together in one company. Some tax reliefs may depend on whether there is a 51 per cent or 75 per cent relationship with the group companies involved.

- **Administration** – the more companies you have, the greater the administrative burden, the greater the cost and the more paper is generated.

- **Complexity** – there can also be a conflict between the way a court will look at a group of companies and the everyday practicalities of running the group: the court will see a number of distinct legal entities, each with its own legal rights and obligations; the executives running the group may view the lot as one business with reporting lines and managerial responsibilities crossing those legal boundaries. Superimposing a different management structure on an existing corporate group structure can cause problems if those boundaries are not respected.

In addition to its definitions of subsidiary and holding company, the Companies Act introduces definitions of 'subsidiary undertaking' and 'parent undertaking'. These are wider definitions used in accounting and encompass not only ordinary subsidiaries and holding companies but also other situations where there is effective control and the accounts of two or more companies should be consolidated. They can also include entities other than companies – such as partnerships and unincorporated associations.

Guarantee and unlimited companies and limited liability partnerships

Companies limited by guarantee are often found in the not-for-profit, charity or non-trading sectors, though there is no restriction on the use to which they can be put. Such companies have guarantors rather than shareholders. These guarantors are members who agree to make a limited contribution towards the payment of the company's debts in the event of winding up. That limit is usually fixed at a nominal £1 and is only required if the company's assets fall short.

A guarantee company may drop the word 'limited' from its name if, but only if, it exists for charitable purposes or to promote other good causes and there is a ban on the payment of any dividends to its members (and, on a winding up, any surplus goes to a body with a similar purpose).

Different again are unlimited companies. Here, the liability of members is truly unlimited and they can be required to pay the company's debts without limit if it defaults and is wound up. Of course, for the shareholders of many small companies the concept of limited liability is at times notional – banks and landlords will often require personal guarantees of a company's liabilities. So an unlimited company may be no more than an acceptance of a reality, and it will carry the big advantage of secrecy: there is generally no obligation to file accounts at Companies House.

Since 2000, there has been an entirely new legal entity – a limited liability partnership. An LLP is often the vehicle used by large firms of lawyers and accountants to enjoy both the tax benefits of a partnership and the limited liability of a company. In most respects, it's more akin to a company than anything else, but legally it's a new concept. The main quid pro quo for limited liability is the obligation to file annual accounts at Companies House.

3. Company constitution

Anyone forming a company puts their name to two documents: a memorandum of association and articles of association. The former is now not much more than a formality; the latter comprises the company's constitution.

Memorandum

The memorandum is now a bald statement that the initial subscriber wishes to form a company and agrees to become a member by taking at least one share. Beyond that, it has no useful purpose.

Up until October 2009, it was all very different. Unlike a natural person, a company did not have complete freedom to do whatever its directors wanted. It was, instead, restricted to those things its memorandum, and more specifically the objects clause of its memorandum, said it could do. Anything else would be ultra vires, that is beyond its proper powers, potentially putting the directors who authorised the offending action in breach of their duties.

All that was swept away by the Companies Act 2006. Now, a company can do anything lawful – unless its articles say otherwise. (In some cases, there will be good cause to be prescriptive. Where a company is a charity, the objects will at least be restricted to a charitable purpose; where a joint venture company is formed, the parties may want to specify the purpose for which they have come together and funded the company.)

Two notes of caution:

■ A company formed before October 2009 will have had the objects clause from its memorandum automatically transferred to the articles. It may not appear on the face of a printed version of the articles, but it will be treated as there by dint of the Companies Act 2006. Shareholders may subsequently have voted to remove it, but if not, it remains and continues to act as a restriction on what the company can do.

■ Even where there is no objects clause, directors need to use their unfettered powers to promote the success of the company, not for some extraneous purpose (see Chapter 2, section 3). So transactions that have no commercial benefit, such as gifts or a guarantee of another's liabilities, might still be vulnerable.

Articles

The articles of association are a company's internal regulations or by-laws. They set out both the way the company is to be run and the rights of its shareholders. It is the articles that deal with subjects such as the benefits attached to each class of share, the quorum for a meeting and the way to transfer shares.

Companies legislation sets out a model form of articles for a private company and for a company limited by guarantee. The latest versions date from October 2009 and are shorter than the previous forms known as Tables A and C respectively. For the first time, there is also a model form of articles for a public company. All are drafted in plain English.

Tempting as it may be to use these model forms, they won't suit every company. The private company articles, in particular, are designed for a small owner/manager enterprise and will not be right for larger companies with more complex ownership structures.

Many older private companies will often still be using the old Table A as the basis for their articles, with a few amendments to suit their particular circumstances. Public companies, by contrast, and some larger private companies, are more likely to dispense with all model forms and instead to set out the entirety of their articles in one bespoke document.

Your articles can say whatever you want, subject to one proviso: you cannot go against the law. For example, the Companies Act says a company can only pay a dividend if it has distributable profits, and the articles cannot improve on that. Similarly, the right of shareholders to remove a director by passing an ordinary resolution must be upheld: the articles can make it easier to get rid of a board member; they cannot make it more difficult.

Stock Exchange or AIM traded companies must comply with certain rules as a condition of being quoted. And if the articles of a fully listed company have any 'unusual features', they must first be approved by the UK Listing Authority (that is, the Financial Services Authority).

It's often said that the articles are a contract between a company and its members. When you become a shareholder you do so subject to the terms of the company's articles – now and in the future. You will have the opportunity to vote on any change, but once the vote has gone through, it will be binding on you, whether you agreed or not. The corollary is that a shareholder can go to court to stop a company acting in a way that is contrary to its articles – the 'contract' binds both sides.

Just as you can put into your articles what you want, you can change them at any time – provided a special resolution is passed (see section 5). Changes, however, will be open to challenge if they cannot be justified as being in good faith or are partisan. If a majority of shareholders are motivated by malice and push through a change harmful to the minority, a court might overturn the change as not being in the interests of the company as a whole.

A company's articles are a public document. They must be filed at Companies House. So they are not the place to put details that a private company might want to keep confidential – a financial return to be enjoyed by a shareholder, for example, or detailed voting arrangements. Shareholders in joint venture companies or in private equity investments might opt to keep these details private. A company's articles, in other words, may not tell the whole story of the relationship between shareholders and their company – other documents, such as a shareholders' agreement, might be needed for the full picture.

Board of directors and board committees

We look in more detail at directors in section 4 below, and at their duties and responsibilities in the next chapter. And in Chapter 4 we look at corporate governance, in which directors have a major role to play. But for now it's worth highlighting one provision found in most articles (using here the wording from the new model articles): 'the directors are responsible for the management of the company's business, for which purpose they may exercise all the powers of the company'.

That encapsulates the directors' authority, the basis for the power they exercise. It protects them, and the company, from interference by shareholders in the day-to-day management of the company. If the shareholders do not like what the directors are doing, they can remove them or, less drastically, pass a special resolution giving them a particular direction. Or they can change the articles to limit the directors' powers. Neither course of action is commonly seen in practice, though an implied threat by shareholders to remove directors can have the desired effect.

Just as shareholders effectively delegate the management of a company to its directors, those directors, acting together as a board, will be permitted by the articles to delegate decision making to individual executive directors and to committees of the main board. Some committees may be a permanent feature, required by governance considerations – for example, remuneration or audit committees – others may be more ad hoc and formed to see through a particular deal or issue (see section 15 of Chapter 4).

Delegation to individual executive directors, or to an executive committee, may be by means of a board resolution. Executives' service contracts may also set out clearly what their duties are and what authority they have.

4. Company personnel

Shareholders

For all companies with a share capital, the terms 'shareholder' and 'member' are interchangeable. But whichever term is used, it will refer to the person who has the legal ownership of a share – that is the person who is shown in the company's register of members as holding the share. That registered shareholder may be the only person with an interest in the share, or may just be a nominee who holds the share for someone else. In the latter case, that someone else is the beneficial owner, who may enjoy the income from the share, decide how the share is voted and receive the sale proceeds when the share is disposed of.

The general rule is that a company has no need to take note of the beneficial owners of its shares or even know who they are (although it may, in certain circumstances, be able to force disclosure of their identity); the company concerns itself only with those persons its register shows as being members.

Keen, however, to 'enhance shareholder engagement', in October 2007 the government gave beneficial owners (including anyone who owns shares through a PEP, ISA or similar vehicle) new rights. Under the Companies Act 2006, they are able to exercise many of the rights attaching to their shares themselves. These include the calling of a shareholder meeting, the receipt of notice of a meeting and the appointment of a proxy (which can be the beneficial owner himself) to cast a vote.

For the rights of beneficial owners to be recognised, there are two provisos:

■ a company's articles must allow for it;

■ the registered shareholder must 'nominate' the beneficial owner who is to enjoy these rights.

If these provisos are not met, it remains the case that only shareholders named in the register can vote, receive dividends and exercise other shareholder rights. And only they can enforce rights against the company; the beneficial owner cannot bring a direct claim.

The shareholders are the owners of the company. They ultimately control what it does by virtue of their ability to remove and appoint directors and to change the articles. Their rights and obligations as shareholders will usually be set out in the articles, backed up by the Companies Act and the law as developed by judges in decided cases.

There may also be a shareholders' agreement that sets out terms agreed between the shareholders; or in a 50:50 company, a joint venture agreement that sets out how deadlocks between shareholders are to be settled. A company that has received private equity or venture capital funding may have an investment agreement that also deals with the rights between various groups of shareholders. But, unlike the articles, these agreements will only bind those shareholders who sign up to them originally or who do so when they become shareholders and put their name to some form of deed of adherence. The articles, by contrast, apply to all who have acquired shares at any time, whether they have specifically agreed to them or not.

Directors

We have looked already at the role directors play as the individuals to whom the management of the company is delegated by shareholders. But who exactly are the directors? Is it just those given the name, or can it include others? There are three categories, as explained below.

- **Companies House** or **registered director** – most directors are clearly appointed by the board or by shareholders, and their details are registered at Companies House. They may be executive or non-executive:

  - An executive director is a director who is also an employee of the company. Their contract of employment will impose specific duties: for example, a finance director will be responsible for the day-to-day management of the company's finances.

  - Non-executive directors, by contrast, are not employees of the company. They will usually have a non-executive appointment letter rather than a contract of employment. That means they are paid fees, not salaries (see Chapter 4 for more on their role). They will usually be part-time and will not be expected to be involved in the day-to-day running of the company. Despite this, there is no legal distinction between them and executive directors. Many of the duties placed on them will be the same.

- **De facto director** – the Companies Act 2006 says that 'director' includes 'any person occupying the position of director, by whatever name called'. So you might be called 'governor' or 'trustee' and actually be a director. Conversely, a director of sales or HR director might not be a member of the board at all. It's the role you perform, not the title you're given, that determines whether you're a director or not. If you turn up to directors' meetings and speak, and vote, as if you were a director, you run the risk that the courts will treat you as having all the duties and liabilities described in this book.

- **Shadow director** – defined as a 'person in accordance with whose directions or instructions the directors of a company are accustomed to act'. Note that the shadow director's influence has to be over the whole board, or at least a majority of it, not just one or two directors; and there has to be some history of influence, not just an isolated occurrence. Professional advisers, such as lawyers and accountants, are specifically excluded, as are parent companies in certain circumstances. But a dominant individual at the parent, company doctors sent in to implement a corporate recovery plan, and even banks seeking to protect their loans to a company, are potential shadow directors.

In contrast with the first two categories, not every reference in companies legislation to a director covers a shadow director as well: there must be specific wording to include a shadow director. Most significantly, a shadow director can, like the others, be liable for wrongful trading when a company becomes insolvent (see section 3 of Chapter 10).

In many smaller companies, directors will continue in office until they voluntarily resign or are forcibly removed. Larger companies and all listed companies will require directors to retire at the AGM (for example, a third or even all of the directors might retire each year), and directors newly appointed by the board must retire at the following AGM. They then stand for re-election, when shareholders usually vote them back in.

At the time of writing, the Financial Reporting Council was seeking views as to whether the UK Corporate Governance Code should recommend the annual election of the entire board or of just the chairman (see section 14 of Chapter 4).

A number of people are barred from being directors:

■ Undischarged bankrupts;

■ Individuals under the age of 16;

■ Those disqualified from acting as a director under the Company Directors Disqualification Act 1986 for persistent breaches of company law, following a conviction for fraud or for committing other offences. Most orders under the Act result from a company insolvency, or a director's obvious 'unfitness' to be concerned in the management of a company. Ignoring a disqualification order is a criminal offence carrying a two-year prison sentence.

Further restrictions may be imposed by the articles of association; it used, for example, to be common for the articles to require a director to hold shares in the company.

The 2006 Companies Act removed the rule that directors of a public company had to stand down when they reached 70; from April 2007, there has been no upper age limit.

Corporate Directors

A director does not have to be an individual. A company can serve as a director on the board of another company. The use of 'corporate directors' is, however, curtailed under the Companies Act 2006, which requires every company to have at least one individual or, in legal parlance, 'natural person' on the board.

Corporate directors can be represented at board meetings by different people at different times. They can also be used to distance individuals from liability (though it's questionable how effective a device that is). In any event, the Act requires at least one individual as a director, so there will always be one person of flesh and blood on the board who is personally accountable for its failings.

Company secretary

As stated in section 2, all public companies must have a secretary. Private companies have been able to drop the role since April 2008, but many choose to retain the post where there is a real job to be done.

The increasing focus in recent years on corporate governance means the role of the company secretary has grown in importance. In many ways, the secretary is now seen as the guardian of the company's proper compliance with both the law and best practice. Chapter 3 goes into more detail.

Auditors

Companies above a certain minimum size are required to have auditors who, each year, examine and report on the company's accounts and confirm whether they comply with companies legislation and whether they give a 'true and fair view' of the company. Many smaller companies are relieved of this requirement, though they must still prepare and file accounts.

A detailed description of the duties of an auditor is beyond the scope of this chapter, but it is worth noting that if the auditor fails in its duties it may be liable for any loss the failure has caused, both to the company and to its shareholders. In some cases, it may also be liable to third parties who have relied on the audit report – though recent case law has provided some limit on auditors' exposure.

When companies fail and investors are looking for someone with deep pockets to compensate them for their losses, it's often the auditors who are in the firing line. The 2008 banking crisis, the collapse of Arthur Andersen after the Enron scandal, and Equitable Life's multi-million pound claim against Ernst and Young (albeit unsuccessful), are all good examples of auditors under pressure for their perceived failures.

The potential claims are now so big, and the risks of losing one of the remaining 'Big Four' firms so catastrophic, that from April 2008 auditors have been able to agree with a company each year a cap on their liability for the audit. But there are several hurdles to be overcome – not only must the finance director agree, but the shareholders must also approve the limitation at the AGM. Even then, when any claim against the auditors comes to court, the judge can substitute a higher amount if that would be 'fair and reasonable'.

Despite pressure from the auditing profession and from government, companies and their investors have proved unenthusiastic for the change. Indeed, at the time of writing, no major listed company has yet even asked shareholders to vote on such a limitation. Opposition from US regulators has also been significant in the case of companies with dual listings in New York.

Given the importance of their role, the hiring and firing of auditors is also closely regulated. The directors appoint the first auditors of a company and can fill any vacancy that arises between general meetings. Apart from that, the auditors are appointed by a resolution of shareholders at each annual general meeting, and there are special notice provisions (see section 5) where a new auditor is to be appointed in place of the firm appointed at the previous AGM.

An auditor can be removed by ordinary resolution of the shareholders, but, again, there are special safeguards in the legislation that have to be observed.

A resigning auditor must produce a statement setting out any circumstances connected with the resignation that should be brought to shareholders' attention. Alternatively, if there are no such circumstances, that fact must be stated. This is designed to prevent auditors who are unhappy with any aspect of the accounts departing quietly and keeping the problems to themselves. Concerns must be stated frankly. Additional safeguards aim to protect the company from the risk of defamatory material being circulated.

Auditors will always rightly point out that they do not prepare the accounts on which they report: that is the job of the directors. In practice, though, they may help smaller companies put the accounts together – as a general rule, the smaller the business, the greater their assistance.

The accountancy firms provide numerous services to their clients above and beyond the basic audit. Governance principles suggest that the auditor might have a conflict of interest in doing commercial work in addition to its audit duties (see section 16 of Chapter 4), and statute requires that details of non-audit services are disclosed in the annual report. At the same time, however, the involvement of auditors has been extended with the requirement for them to check some of the factual information in the directors' remuneration report (see Chapter 7).

5. Company meetings

Board meetings

As we've seen above, the articles will delegate the management of the company to its board of directors. The board will act collectively, meeting regularly to consider and decide issues affecting the company. How those board meetings are run is a matter largely for the articles and for the board itself to decide. Unlike shareholders' meetings, which are more tightly regulated, board meetings are generally free of legislative interference.

So there is nothing in statute about the notice to be given for board meetings. Any director or the secretary can call a board meeting and, unless the articles or a previous board meeting have stipulated the length of notice to be given, the only requirement is that it be reasonable.

What's reasonable will depend on the type of company and its past practice. For a private company where all directors are already on site, reasonable notice may be a few hours or even minutes; unless the articles or a board resolution say anything to the contrary, the notice can be written or oral and need not detail an agenda for the meeting. For a large international company with directors scattered over the globe and non-executives with other responsibilities, regular board meetings will be fixed a year or more ahead, with detailed papers sent out well in advance.

That's the legal position, but there's a clear contrast here with what today would be regarded as best practice. As Chapter 4 describes, the UK Corporate Governance Code for listed companies says that boards should meet regularly, that there should be a schedule of matters that may only be settled by the board, and that directors should be properly briefed. (The ICSA website has further guidance on this.) In addition, the Code requires that the directors' annual report contains a record of attendance at board and committee meetings.

The articles will usually stipulate a minimum number of directors to form a quorum before the meeting can go ahead. But it's important to realise that:

- Having a quorum is not a substitute for giving notice of a meeting. Achieving a quorum will not validate a board meeting if reasonable notice has not first been given to all directors.

- When calculating the quorum, the articles will need to be checked: they will often exclude a director who has a personal interest in the matter under consideration (see section 4 of Chapter 2).

Votes at a board meeting will be calculated on the basis of one for each director present, with the chairman having a casting vote in the event of a tie, unless the articles provide for anything different. A director excluded from the quorum because of a personal interest in a matter will also be excluded from voting.

If the articles are well drafted, board meetings by telephone or video conference will be permitted. And for smaller companies, board resolutions may often be in writing, signed by all the directors entitled to receive notice.

Where a meeting is held, there is a legal requirement that minutes are taken (and the Companies Act 2006 requires them to be retained for at least 10 years). Minutes allow a director to have their views on a matter recorded – something that can be useful if questions are raised in the future, particularly after an insolvency (see section 2 of Chapter 10). Minutes can also act as evidence of the factors taken into account by the board when reaching a decision (see the box on decision taking and record keeping in Chapter 2, page 29).

The board can delegate matters to sub-committees, and listed companies are required by the Corporate Governance Code to have audit, remuneration and nomination committees. Resolutions establishing committees may dictate quorum, notice and other requirements; failing that, they will follow the same rules as for the full board.

Annual General Meeting

A public company must hold an annual general meeting within six months of its year end. (Listed companies have to publish their report and accounts within four months, so in practice will call an AGM within that period.)

The time and place of the AGM are matters for the board to decide, but, given that the AGM is a rare opportunity for shareholders to have their say and to question directors publicly, companies have faced criticism when they've opted for times and venues that make it difficult for many shareholders to attend.

Under the Companies Act 2006, a private company does not have to hold an AGM, though it can if it wants (and, indeed, may still be required to do so by an old set of articles).

The Corporate Governance Code states that the chairmen of the board's audit, remuneration and nomination committees should be sure to attend the meeting so that they can answer relevant questions from shareholders. Shareholder attendance at AGMs is, however, usually very low, with many choosing to vote by proxy on the standard resolutions to be proposed, or not to vote at all.

Periodic furore at directors' pay packages, and the requirement that the directors' remuneration report be put to shareholders for approval, can sometimes lead to increased numbers at AGMs, and some consequent flexing of shareholder muscle.

The main purpose of most AGMs, though, is for the directors 'to lay before the company in general meeting' the previous year's audited accounts and accompanying reports. Note the wording here – there is no requirement that shareholders approve the accounts or accept them. Shareholders have no ability to reject the accounts. They must stand as they are, having been prepared by the directors and audited by the auditors. A public company AGM simply provides the opportunity for the directors to present the accounts; the resolution put to shareholders will usually be 'to receive' the accounts and reports.

Apart from the accounts, usual business at the AGM will comprise the declaration of any dividend proposed by the board, the appointment of auditors and the fixing of their fees (the latter task usually being delegated to the board), and the election of any directors who are retiring because the articles say they must (see section on directors, above).

Listed companies will also commonly propose resolutions at the AGM to:

■ give directors authority to allot shares, up to a certain limit;

■ disapply pre-emption rights on the issue of shares, up to a certain limit;

■ renew authority for the company to buy up to 10 per cent of its own shares;

■ approve the directors' remuneration report;

■ allow shareholder meetings (other than an AGM) to be called on 14 clear days' notice.

The AGM is not restricted to this business and, in addition, will often be used to put to shareholders resolutions to amend the articles, adopt new incentive schemes or do anything else that requires their approval.

Shareholders can propose their own resolutions for an AGM but they have to act in sufficient numbers: there must either be at least 100 of them holding a certain amount of paid up share capital, or enough of them to represent at least five per cent of the votes.

Other general meetings

If something requires shareholder approval and cannot wait until the next AGM, a general meeting of shareholders can be called (known as an extraordinary general meeting until the Companies Act 2006 dropped the term). Usually, it will be the directors who convene the meeting, but the shareholders can force the directors' hand if they collectively own at least one-tenth of the paid-up voting share capital (one-twentieth in certain circumstances). If the board then fails to comply within 21 days, shareholders can go ahead and call the meeting themselves.

As with AGMs, the directors must act in good faith when convening a general meeting and should avoid picking a time and place with the intention of making it difficult for shareholders to attend.

Many private companies with a small number of shareholders will have no need to hold general meetings – where a shareholder vote is needed, a written resolution can be used (see below).

Notice

All shareholders are entitled to receive written notice of a meeting unless the articles say otherwise. In addition, notice of a general meeting must also be given to each director (whether a shareholder or not). Older articles may also require it to be sent to the auditors – a point that can often be missed.

Notice can be given to shareholders in hard-copy form, electronically or via a website. Whichever method is chosen, it's important that the relevant provisions in the Companies Act and the articles are followed: failure to do so can invalidate the notice, the meeting and the resolutions passed at it.

Documents and information to be sent to shareholders can be posted on a website if a shareholder resolution allowing this has been passed (or the articles permit it). Shareholders can opt out and still require hard copies through the post. In any event, each time a document is put on the website shareholders must be told, usually by hard-copy letter.

E-mail can be used to send notices and other documents where a shareholder has specifically agreed to that method. (See the box on electronic communication with shareholders in Chapter 3.)

Where a notice is sent through the mail, the Companies Act stipulates that it will be deemed to have been received 48 hours after posting, excluding weekends and bank holidays, unless a company's articles have a different rule. An AGM for a public company requires 21 clear days' notice; all other meetings – a private company AGM (if held) and all other general meetings – only need 14 clear days. (In the case of listed company general meetings, the 14 days has to be approved at each year's AGM; otherwise it's 21 days.) For these purposes, 'clear days' means exclusive of the day on which the notice is deemed served and the day of the meeting.

An example will explain the way this works: a plc AGM notice may be posted on 1 July. If the articles state that notices sent by post are served 48 hours later, notice will be deemed given on 3 July. Day 1 of the notice period will then be 4 July; day 21 will be 24 July, which means that the meeting can be held on 25 July. If weekends and bank holidays are to be excluded, the notice period can be longer by eight days or more.

For listed companies, the Corporate Governance Code requires the AGM notice and related papers to be sent to shareholders at least 20 working days before the meeting.

The notice must give sufficient indication of the business of the meeting, so that a shareholder can decide whether to attend or not. This will usually be achieved by setting out in full the resolutions to be proposed at the meeting; and, for special resolutions, the full text must be given. The notice must also tell shareholders that they can appoint a proxy to attend and vote in their place.

These notice periods can be dispensed with if, in the case of a private company, agreement is given by those holding at least 90 per cent of the nominal value of the voting shares. For a public company, that figure goes up to 95 per cent, and for a plc's AGM all shareholders must agree.

Special notice

In two specific situations 'special notice' may be required:

■ removing an auditor and appointing an auditor where there has been a change since the last AGM;

■ removing a director.

Special notice is a commonly misunderstood concept. Special notice is not given by the company, but to the company by a shareholder.

Notice to move the relevant resolution must be given to the company at least 28 days before the meeting. Having received the special notice, the company must inform shareholders of the resolution when it gives notice of the meeting.

Shareholder circulars

Anything other than the routine AGM resolutions is likely to require some form of explanation to shareholders by the board in the form of a letter or circular. In the case of a listed company, the Listing Rules contain requirements for such a circular. For example, the directors must say whether they believe the proposal is in the best interests of shareholders as a whole, and they must recommend which way shareholders should vote.

Unless the circular is dealing with standard business of the type described in the Listing Rules, it must be submitted to the UK Listing Authority for approval before it's sent to shareholders.

Resolutions

There are three types of resolution, each with a different purpose and distinct requirements.

- ■ **Ordinary** – unless companies legislation or the articles require anything different, an ordinary resolution will be sufficient for all decisions to be taken by general meetings of shareholders. If proposed at a plc AGM, 21 clear days' notice will be necessary; if proposed at a private company AGM or at any other general meeting, only 14 clear days are needed (see the paragraphs above on notice).

  An ordinary resolution will be passed if a simple majority of those shareholders who are present and who vote are in favour. If a poll is called, it needs a simple majority of all the votes cast (one share giving one vote, unless the articles say differently). Note: it's a simple majority of those who vote, not of all shareholders – or even of all who attend the meeting.

- ■ **Special** – matters that are less routine or of more importance, such as changes to the articles of a company, disapplying pre-emption rights on the issue of shares or a switch from being a private to a public company, will require a special resolution. Unless proposed at a public company AGM, 14 clear days' notice of the resolution must be given (if a listed company, the ability to call a meeting on 14 days' notice must be approved at the AGM). The notice must clearly state that a special resolution is to be proposed. To be carried, it needs the support of 75 per cent of those voting or, on a poll, 75 per cent of the votes cast.

- ■ **Written** – shareholders with more than 50 per cent of a private company's shares can agree an ordinary resolution without holding a meeting; for a special resolution, the figure goes up to 75 per cent. As a result, there's little reason ever to hold a shareholder meeting for a private company. The resolution must still be circulated to all shareholders (it's a criminal offence not to do so) but there is no need to get a hard copy signature if a shareholder's agreement is signified in writing in some other way, such as an e-mail.

Shareholders do not have to wait for the directors to propose a resolution: those holding at least five per cent of the votes can require the company to circulate their own resolutions. Any resolution circulated to the shareholders will lapse if it has not been agreed to by the necessary majority within 28 days.

Note that written resolutions cannot be used by public companies.

6. Shares and share issues

A lot has been said about shareholders, but little about the shares they hold.

Share capital

Historically, companies had two kinds of share capital: authorised and issued.

Authorised was the share capital the company had created and the maximum it could issue. A company with a £1m authorised share capital could, for example, have 10 million authorised shares of 10p each.

Issued is the share capital issued and held by shareholders. It may be all 10 million shares in the above example, or only nine million, leaving one million authorised but unissued.

The Companies Act 2006 did away with the concept of authorised share capital, leaving just the shares that have actually been issued. The notion of authorised share capital lives on in only one respect: where it appeared in a company's memorandum before October 2009, it will be deemed to have transferred to the articles and, unless removed by a shareholder vote, will continue to act as a limit on the number of shares that can be issued.

Share values

A share will have a nominal or par value: 1p, 10p, £1 or any other sum in any currency. And it's an absolute rule that a share cannot be issued fully paid for anything less than its nominal value – that is, it cannot be issued at a discount. A company cannot issue a £1 share fully paid for 99p or less. A company thus has no ability to issue free shares (but it may buy shares in the market and give them as free shares to employees, say, as part of an incentive scheme).

A company can, however, issue shares nil or partly paid. That means it can issue a £1 share and take no money for it on issue; or it may issue the share paid as to 25p only. The amount unpaid (the full £1 or the balance of 75p) remains due and will have to be paid when the company calls for payment at a time anticipated in the terms of the share's issue, or on a winding up if the company's assets are not enough to settle its liabilities.

Of course, a £1 share will often be issued with a price being paid to the company well in excess of that sum; the difference between the nominal value and the price paid is the premium. The directors are under a duty in issuing shares (as in all things) to act in the best interests of the company, and if a £1 share has a market value of £1.50, they must have a good reason for issuing it for anything less than £1.50. The nominal value is only the minimum price at which shares can be issued.

Different classes of share

Unless the articles say otherwise, all shares will rank equally. But to the extent they are given different rights – to dividends, to a return of capital on winding up and on voting – they will comprise different classes of share. A company may have one class of share or it may have many.

Ordinary shares are the basic building block of a company's share capital. They will carry votes (usually one each), have a right to a dividend if the directors decide to pay one, and also be entitled to part of any surplus on a winding up of the company. Other shares will take their rights, or lack of them, by reference to this base position. **Non-voting shares** are self-explanatory (and a rarity these days, generally shunned by investing institutions but favoured by companies with a substantial family shareholding – for example, Daily Mail and General Trust). **Preference shares** may have a preferential right to a dividend ahead of the ordinary shares, or to a return of capital, or both. **Deferred shares** will rank behind the ordinaries (and tend to be used in a capital reorganisation where there is a need to make the shares virtually value-less).

Where these different classes of share exist, the rights of each one can only be changed in line with requirements in the articles or, if they are silent, requirements in the Companies Act. The articles will commonly stipulate a certain level of consent to any change; in default, the Act requires the holders of 75 per cent in nominal value to consent in writing, or holders of shares of that class to pass a special resolution (see page 20) approving the change at a separate meeting. Outside investors in a non-listed company may often expand the definition of what amounts to a class right and so prevent certain acts of the company (for example, the payment of a dividend) without their prior consent.

Share issues

Directors cannot issue newly created shares without shareholder authority to do so. Two provisions of the Companies Act 2006 are key here and will be familiar from any listed company AGM notice.

■ **Section 549** stops the directors from issuing shares to anyone unless they are authorised to do so in the articles or by shareholders passing an ordinary resolution. This ban includes an agreement to issue shares and the grant of options that will result in a future issue of shares (although employee share schemes are exempt). Listed companies will ask shareholders to give them this authority each year at the AGM, but will have to respect certain limitations stipulated by institutional shareholders – the rule has been that only one-third of the existing share capital can be issued – and the authority has to be renewed at each AGM.

This rule does not apply to a private company with only one class of share. In that case, the directors are free to issue shares without shareholder consent, unless the articles provide otherwise.

■ **Section 561** obliges a company to offer new shares first of all to its existing shareholders in the same proportions they already hold shares. In other words, it upholds shareholders' right to be protected from dilution. If they are willing to pay the price asked for the new shares, they can have them. But this only applies where the shares are offered for cash – if a company is issuing shares in exchange for shares in another company, say, or in payment for a non-cash asset, there's no requirement to offer the shares to existing shareholders first of all.

The section can be disapplied, along with section 549, either in the articles or by a shareholder vote, though only by a special resolution.

Again, institutional shareholders have their price: only shares equal to five per cent of the issued share capital can be issued without first offering them to shareholders.

Rights issues and bonus issues

A **rights issue** is a common way for a company to raise fresh capital: it issues new shares, offering them first to its existing shareholders. Indeed, section 561, discussed above, obliges a company to treat any issue of shares for cash as a rights issue unless the shareholders have first agreed otherwise. (A rights issue for a listed company will often not follow this procedure because of various practical difficulties and the additional requirements of the Listing Rules.)

A listed company rights issue will usually offer shares at a discount to the current market price, sometimes a heavy discount if the shareholders' appetite for the shares needs to be stimulated. That discount means that there is an inherent value in the right to be offered the shares, and the shareholders in a listed company can trade those rights and realise that value if they do not want to take up the shares themselves.

Alternatives to a rights issue include an **open offer** where shareholders are invited to subscribe for a number of new shares based on their proportionate entitlements. This can be less complex than a rights issue but it does not give shareholders the opportunity to trade their rights to take up shares and so benefit from the discount. A **vendor placing** may also be used as part of a transaction to buy another company. Shares are allotted by the purchaser to the sellers of the target but the purchaser's investment bank agrees to find investors or placees who will take those shares and so give the sellers cash. Institutional shareholders of the purchaser may insist on a clawback, whereby those shares are first offered to them in proportion to their existing holdings.

A **bonus issue** involves no new money. Also called a **capitalisation or scrip issue**, it takes a sum from the company's reserves (distributable profits that could be used to pay a dividend, or the share premium account) and capitalises it by using it to pay for the new shares. The issued share capital is increased without any new money being invested. The new shares are issued to existing shareholders pro rata to their shareholdings and so no dilution occurs.

2

Duties

There's no doubt that directors' legal duties are onerous and that the penalties for breaching them can be stiff (see section 5 below). But it's important to remember that there is no expectation of perfection or infallibility. The overriding legal requirement is to act honestly, competently and conscientiously.

Provided directors have a proper understanding of their role and take basic protective measures, the risks of committing a breach of duty can be kept to an acceptable level.

In this chapter, we explain some of the legal duties owed by a director and examine the code of directors' duties in the Companies Act 2006.

1. The nature of the fiduciary relationship

Many of the duties imposed under the law arise because the director acts as a fiduciary for the shareholders of the company. A fiduciary is someone who exercises powers or holds money or assets on behalf of others. Thus, the trustee of a family trust is a fiduciary for the beneficiaries; a solicitor holding money for a client is a fiduciary for that client.

The law and the judges provide protection for those on whose behalf fiduciaries act, by placing duties on the fiduciary and imposing sanctions when the duties are breached.

Directors should always see themselves as custodians of the company: its assets are not theirs to deal with solely as they wish. Like the trustee, they are holding and managing assets on behalf of beneficiaries, in their case, the shareholders.

2. The extent of a director's power and authority

Directors do not have unlimited powers to run a company on behalf of the shareholders. They may only exercise the powers granted to them either by the general law or by the company's constitution (the articles of association – see Chapter 1, section 3). For that reason, most companies will have an article on the lines of: 'the directors are responsible for the management of the company's business, for which purpose they may exercise all the powers of the company'.

Unless specific powers and authority have been delegated to a named director, it will usually be the case that powers can only be exercised by the board of directors acting together as a body.

Directors should be aware that when they delegate any of their duties to others, including the company secretary, the responsibility and liability for fulfilling those duties remains with them. Delegation and abdication are not the same thing. Directors need periodically to satisfy themselves that the secretary or other delegate is carrying out his or her tasks properly and that all legal requirements are being met. And warning signs to the contrary should be acted on.

3. The code of directors' duties

Before the Companies Act 2006, the law on directors' duties was in places uncertain, contradictory and anachronistic. It was ripe for reform, and the code of directors' duties, contained in the Act, was the government's response. This streamlined and clarified the old rules but was more than a consolidation or simplification of what had gone before. There were some subtle changes to the rules, and Parliament introduced a new concept: 'enlightened shareholder value'.

The old formula was clear that a director's primary duties were to the company and its shareholders. There was an ineffectual reference to employees, and creditors always took precedence on insolvency, but the law was settled that a director should act in the best interests of all shareholders, and that included future shareholders. With the Companies Act 2006, directors were required to consider other concerns that may affect a company's success. The focus for directors shifted from looking solely at shareholders' interests: enlightened shareholder value means taking account of other stakeholders as well.

The code of directors' duties applies to all companies, public and private, holding and subsidiary (and is not to be confused with the UK Corporate Governance Code, which applies only to listed companies – see Chapter 4). It needs to be understood by all directors and by the level of management who report to and work with the board.

There are seven duties in all. We look at the first four below; the remaining three, concerned with conflicts of interest, are examined in the next section.

Duty to act within your powers

As we have seen, directors have the job of managing the company and they are given certain powers to enable them to do that. But they must act according to the company's constitution and use those powers in the interests of the company, not to further their own narrow interests. So, for example, their power to issue new shares must be used for the purpose of raising capital for the business. Issuing shares to your cronies just to keep voting control in friendly hands is an abuse of power and a breach of duty.

Duty to promote the success of the company

The 2006 Act subtly re-cast the old law, which imposed a duty to act in good faith in the best interests of the company as a whole. Now, a director of a company must act in the way they consider, in good faith, would be most likely to promote the success of the company for the benefit of its members as a whole.

Lawyers in 2006 might have worried about how you define 'success', but the reality was that there was no practical difference between this wording and the old duty to act in the 'best interests' of the company. The change lay, instead, in the addition of the principle of 'enlightened shareholder value' and the idea that the interests of other stakeholders, not just those of shareholders, need to be considered.

To fulfil their duty to promote the success of the company, the legislation requires directors, in reaching their decisions, to have regard to six factors that demonstrate what the government has called 'responsible business behaviour'. These six factors are described in the box on pages 28–29.

Note the wording here: 'have regard to' is key. There is no requirement that any one factor is given precedence over another, that employees must be favoured over the environment, for example, or the community over customers. The final decision might discount all six factors – but the board needs to be able to demonstrate that, where relevant, it has at least considered them and taken them into account.

The success of the company remains the paramount concern for directors. The legislation prompts the board to think about these different factors, but they must remain subsidiary to the over-arching requirement the directors have to act in the way they believe, in good faith, is most likely to promote the company's success. (Where a company is set up for other purposes than to benefit its shareholders – where it's a charity, for example – you can substitute that other purpose.)

The requirement to take these six factors into account where they have a bearing on the matter under consideration has implications for decision taking and record keeping, and these are examined briefly in the box on pages 29–30. Most companies, in any event, will consider these factors, or something like them, as a matter of good practice. The duty merely gives statutory force to something that responsible boards of directors will be doing anyway. (See the case studies on pages 30–31.)

Responsible Business Behaviour

The six factors that boards cannot ignore

As part of its decision-making process, a board needs to consider the following factors and weigh up their influence on its overriding **duty to promote the company's success**.

Of course, some of the six factors will be more relevant than others; much depends on the type of decision being made. There is no requirement to waste time considering the environment and your suppliers where they are clearly unconnected to the matter at hand.

By the same token, some decisions will require the board to have 'regard to' other things as well. The list is not exclusive; it is a prompt, a guide for the 'thinking' board.

■ **The likely long-term consequences of any decision.** Promoting a long-term investment culture was a key objective of the government in introducing the Companies Act 2006. Some companies may find themselves with share registers made up of hedge funds and active value investors who look only for short-term returns. Despite that, the relevance of the long view is something a board is required to consider.

■ **The interests of employees.** Directors have been required to pay regard to employees' interests for many years, though employees have had no direct means of enforcing this duty. That has not changed and, in any event, the interests of employees can diverge. In the unhappy circumstances where the directors have to choose between shutting factory A or factory B, the law gives them no help in deciding between one group of employees and another.

■ **The need to foster business relationships with suppliers, customers and others.** This may seem a statement of the obvious; it's a poor company indeed that's not aware of the importance of this. Nonetheless, small suppliers of large supermarkets may be one group glad of the statutory requirement.

■ **The impact of the company's operations on the community and the environment.** Few large companies now feel they can ignore the environment (see the story of Shell's Brent Spar episode in the box on page 31), but the 'community' is perhaps a trickier concept. The issue may be obvious where one company dominates a town and provides much of the employment and local wealth, but it may not be so clear-cut where the interests of one community conflict with another.

■ **The desirability of maintaining a reputation for high standards of business conduct.** Corporate buccaneers, in other words, have to think twice.

■ **The need to act fairly between members.** This is old law, but remains good under the Companies Act 2006. The private shareholder with a few hundred shares is entitled to the same treatment as the institution with many millions of shares. The disclosure obligations of listed companies make the same point on the dissemination of inside information (see Chapter 5).

All this becomes irrelevant when a company is insolvent, then the interests of creditors take precedence over all else – see Chapter 10.

Decision Taking and Record Keeping: Directors' Self-Defence

The requirement under the code of duties to pay regard to six specific factors of responsible business behaviour (see the previous box) inevitably raised fears of more paperwork. If the law required directors to have regard to these six factors in reaching their decisions, and threatened consequences for them if they did not (see section 5), then surely they'd be wise to keep detailed records of their compliance.

The government, which promoted the Companies Act 2006 as a

way of cutting red tape, was keen to play down the idea. The attorney general tried to reassure: 'There is nothing in this Bill that says there is a need for a paper trail ... I do not agree ... that directors will be subject to a breach if they cannot demonstrate that they have considered every element.'

Nonetheless, directors who have to defend themselves against allegations that they ignored, say, the interests of employees or the community, will need some evidence in their favour.

An attempt at a solution to this problem was made by the GC100, a group of in-house lawyers and company secretaries at FTSE 100 companies who published guidance on the point. They argued that best practice should be for management to prepare a background paper when a board is asked to make a decision of any importance. That paper would deal with all relevant factors (and ignore any that are not). And it would then be up to the directors to read their briefing papers and to use their judgment in arriving at a decision.

That is a practical answer. Minutes do not need to reprise a lengthy boardroom debate weighing up competing factors. The proper place for a consideration of those issues is the board paper circulated ahead of the meeting. That will be good evidence that the directors have complied with their duty to consider all relevant factors.

The solution also highlights the need for management below board level, who prepare the board paper, to have an equally good understanding of directors' duties.

The Duty to Promote the Success of the Company – Case Studies

Two examples that pre-date the Companies Act 2006 serve to illustrate the kind of thinking the government expects from directors. In the first, the board came to the right conclusion first time; in the second, external events led to a re-assessment and a change of heart.

Manchester United

In 2005, Malcolm Glazer was close to succeeding in his bid for Manchester United. But although his offer of 300p a share was generally thought to be fair, the board held off from advising shareholders to accept. Having looked at the Glazer business plan and his method of financing the bid with many millions of debt, they concluded that a takeover on those terms would place a 'significant financial strain on the business', and, in their view, that was not in the company's best interests.

Shareholders are free to act in their own financial interests and most takeovers are decided in favour of the highest bid. But here, in deciding whether to recommend the bid or not, the board looked beyond the current shareholders and focused instead on the interests of the company as a separate entity made up of future as well as current shareholders, and of creditors and employees as well. A company over-burdened with debt was not in their interests. In a foreshadowing of the Act, the board preferred the long-term consequences for the company over the short-term benefit for shareholders.

The last word, though, went to the shareholders. They chose to take the money, as was their prerogative, and so Glazer won the battle.

Shell

The story of the Brent Spar incident shows what can happen when directors fail to think about the wider implications of business decisions.

In 1995 Shell decommissioned its Brent Spar oil storage installation in the North Sea. It had no more use for it and, having taken expert advice, decided that the best solution was to tow it out to the mid-Atlantic and sink it.

Public outrage ensued. Greenpeace occupied the Spar, 50 Shell service stations in Germany were damaged by protesters, two were fire-bombed, and the German chancellor made a formal protest to the British prime minister.

As it saw its carefully nurtured reputation begin to shatter, Shell was forced to re-think. It halted the disposal, revised the plan and came up with an alternative – the offending hulk was recycled as the base for a roll-on/roll-off ferry quay at Mekjarvik in Norway.

Although the original disposal plan seemed to be the best option for Shell, looked at in narrow commercial terms, that was not enough. The company came to realise that a rigorous assessment of the environmental, social and health impact of any major project was equally necessary for its long-term success.

Duty to exercise independent judgment

A director is on the board to act in the best interests of the company as a whole, not to represent the interests of just one shareholder or even a group of like-minded investors. That rule applies irrespective of the circumstances in which the director has been appointed.

In a company set up as a joint venture between two businesses, each shareholder will commonly have the right to appoint an equal number of directors. Similarly, a private equity investor will often put a director on the board to safeguard its investment. But in each case those directors risk trouble if they are seen to act only in the narrow interests of the shareholder who appointed them. Their duty is to the company as a whole and to all the shareholders in the company. A director must not be a 'plant' or a partisan.

Nor can directors 'fetter their discretion', which means they can't give away their decision-making role. Of course, they can sign agreements that commit the company to a particular course of action, and they can do anything that the articles authorise them to do, but as a general rule they can't delegate their powers without the ability to take them back or to change their mind.

Duty to exercise reasonable care, skill and diligence

The law requires a director to use reasonable care, skill and diligence in carrying out their tasks.

What does this mean in terms of brainpower, time commitment, the attention you give the job? No directorship is a sinecure or an honorary position; it's a 'proper' job, requiring a reasonable input, even from an unpaid non-executive.

The Act sets out a double test. First, there is an objective standard: a board member must have the knowledge, skill and experience that would reasonably be expected of anyone doing that job. Second, a subjective standard must also be met: a director has to perform according to the knowledge, skill and experience they actually have.

So there is a basic level of competence that will be expected from all board members; but there is also a higher standard expected of those with some special skill or experience. A qualified accountant doing the job of finance director, for example, will be judged against the standard of a fellow professional with a detailed understanding of the company's finances. Any director with particular knowledge or experience will be expected to use those attributes for the company's benefit and, to that extent, will be judged by a higher standard.

A non-executive director may not have day-to-day knowledge of the company's business and will not see all of the information available to management, but they will have a broader experience and will be expected to use that to probe and challenge their executive colleagues. Just like them, they will also be expected to bring relevant professional skills and qualifications to bear. That is why a board's audit committee is expected to have at least one member with relevant financial experience.

4. Duties relating to conflicts of interest

Directors' obligations to the company must not clash with other interests they may have, or with obligations they owe to others. Transparency in their dealings and relationships is vital. These are the principles behind the statutory duties described in this section.

As with the other directors' duties, the Companies Act 2006 codified the old law on conflicts of interest, replacing some of the (at times) confusing judge-made law with new rules set down in statute.

Avoiding a 'situational' conflict

A director must avoid a situation in which he or she:

> has, or can have, a direct or indirect interest that conflicts, or possibly may conflict, with the interests of the company.

This is very broad drafting, covering both actual and potential conflicts and direct and indirect interests. It applies both to a conflict of interest and a conflict of duty, so it may catch:

■ having an interest in a commercial opportunity that could also be exploited by the company – if you are a director of a property development company, for example, working on similar projects for your own benefit can give rise to a conflict;

■ a director's use for their own purpose of information belonging to the company;

■ a director who sits on two boards where the duties to each may conflict – even a parent and its subsidiary company can have different interests, and the parties to a joint venture may not have the same interests as their joint venture vehicle.

It is these 'situations' that can amount to a breach of duty, not any specific transaction that may arise from them (but see below for 'transactional' conflicts).

At first sight, these rules seem to threaten paralysis on the board. How can directors avoid such conflicts without decision-making grinding to a halt?

Fortunately, there is some relief. There is no breach of duty:

■ if the situation cannot 'reasonably be regarded as likely to give rise to a conflict' – if the director's potential interest is so indirect or remote that no reasonable person would see a problem, it can be ignored; or

■ it has been authorised by the rest of the board. (Note that the interested director cannot vote or be counted in the quorum when deciding whether to authorise or not.)

The articles need to be checked on this latter point. Only the board of a private company incorporated on or after 1 October 2008 is able to authorise a director's conflict without its articles making special provision to that effect. Private companies formed before that date, and all plcs, need to have specific powers in their articles to do so.

The board's authorisation will apply indefinitely but if the nature of the interest changes, a new authorisation will be needed.

If neither get-out is available, the director must avoid the conflict, which may mean giving up the 'other' interest or, alternatively, stepping down from the board.

Disclosing a 'transactional' conflict

If the basic principle is that a company and a director should not have conflicting interests, it must follow that there should be restrictions on them entering into a contract with each other.

When a company is entering into a contract (or any other transaction or arrangement), a director must disclose any interest they have in the contract, whether direct or indirect, **before** the contract is signed. The disclosure must be full and frank so that, before the board approves the contract, it is aware of the nature and extent of the director's interest.

Again, the company's articles need to be checked. They may stipulate that the interested director cannot vote on the matter, or even that shareholder approval is required.

A director can declare an interest in a proposed contract orally at a board meeting, or in a written statement, sent to each director (in hard or soft copy form) before the meeting. Where there is a continuing interest, perhaps as a shareholder or director of a regular supplier or customer, the director can give a general notice saying that they are to be regarded as having an interest in any transaction or arrangement entered into with that other company. If, once made, the declaration becomes inaccurate, it must be updated.

No declaration is needed where:

■ the director was not aware of their own interest (and that lack of awareness was reasonable);

■ the director was not aware of the transaction or arrangement with the company (and that lack of awareness was reasonable);

■ the interest cannot reasonably be regarded as giving rise to a conflict;

■ the rest of the board is already aware of the director's interest (or ought to be aware of it);

■ the interest arises from the director's service contract – a contract that has either already been considered by the board or a board committee or is due to go before them.

Those are the rules for contracts under discussion. What about contracts that already exist? What if a contract, arrangement or transaction has already been concluded but a director later becomes aware that they have an interest in it? Supposing a director new to the board discovers they have an interest in one (or more) of the company's contracts? In these circumstances, a declaration must be made 'as soon as reasonably practicable'. The requirements for the declaration will be similar, and the same exemptions will apply.

Note that, unlike the other duties described here, failure to declare an interest in an existing contract is a criminal offence, punishable by a fine.

Where the contract between the company and a director involves an asset above a certain value, shareholder approval will be needed – see section 6 below.

Accepting benefits from third parties

Taking a bribe from a supplier is clearly wrong. But what about accepting an invitation to Wimbledon or Ascot? Where do you draw the line between fostering good relations with contractors and feathering your own nest or compromising your own integrity?

The Companies Act says that a director must not accept a benefit from a third party that was offered because of the director's position or because of anything they may do or not do as a director.

If a large contract is up for tender, the director who will make the decision should not accept hospitality or a gift from one of the potential bidders. There is no need to show that the company has suffered harm: it is the director's acceptance of the benefit and the reason it was offered that are key.

A director is free to accept the benefit if no reasonable person would see it as giving rise to a conflict, but that may not always be an easy call to make. Having a company policy on the acceptance of gifts and hospitality will help set an appropriate standard.

5. Remedies where there is a breach

If a director breaches any of the duties described in sections 3 and 4, what are the consequences?

Claims by the company

The company itself can bring a claim against the erring director if it can show that it has suffered some loss. If the director has made some personal profit, they can be required to surrender the gain to the company.

A contract or other arrangement entered into by the director in breach of a duty will be void, though it may be open to the company to ratify the agreement if it wishes to do so.

The company may also seek:

■ an injunction to stop the director from carrying out or continuing with the breach;

■ damages by way of compensation;

■ restoration of the company's property;

■ the rescinding of a contract in which the director had an undisclosed interest.

Claims by a company are often retrospective, brought by members of a new board against their predecessors. (It is, after all, unlikely that a board will choose to sue itself: turkeys don't vote for Christmas.) In 2002, for example, the newly installed directors of Equitable Life voted to pursue the company's former directors for the losses it had suffered as a result of problems with its guaranteed income policies. It was only after several years of crippling litigation, which pushed a number of the defendants towards bankruptcy, that the company agreed to withdraw its claims.

Errant directors can also face claims against them when a company is sold. The new owners may appoint new directors and, if things go wrong, they may cast around for past breaches of duty and the opportunity to hold the old directors to account.

Claims by a liquidator or administrator

Once a company becomes insolvent, a liquidator or administrator will be under a duty to consider a claim against a director where a breach of duty is discovered. A claim will be treated as an asset of the company: it will be pursued and realised for the benefit of creditors.

Shareholder claims

A director owes their duties direct to the company, and only the company can complain of any breach. Shareholders have no right to claim against a director for any loss they believe they may have suffered as a result of breach of duty. However much their shares have dropped in price, they cannot recover that loss of value from the directors they hold responsible.

But because few companies will bring a claim against one of their own directors, the law has, over the years, developed a mechanism that allows shareholders to force the company to seek redress. With the permission of the court, shareholders can bring a claim against a director in the name of the company. The claim is initiated and run by shareholders, but it is brought in the company's name and to recover the company's loss.

The distinction is important: the shareholder is not claiming in their own name for their own loss; rather, they are claiming in the company's name for the company's loss. It follows that any sum recovered goes to the company (and it will be the board's decision whether to pass the benefit on to shareholders by way of dividend).

These principles were established over 150 years or so by judges deciding the cases before them. The Companies Act 2006 tidied up the rules under the heading 'derivative claims', the technical term for this type of legal proceeding (see the following box).

Derivative Claims: More Power to the Shareholder?

Derivative claims by shareholders against directors are not new, but setting the rules out in legislation for the first time (in the Companies Act 2006) raised their profile. This led to fears that:

■ activist shareholders (perhaps with experience of the US courts) seeking to persuade a board to sell a business or enter into a merger would use the claims as a tactical device to put pressure on nervous directors;

■ directors, facing the threat of personal liability for some imagined wrong, would quickly accept whatever the loudest shareholder called for.

With various safeguards built in to the procedure for making a claim, those fears have not been realised. To summarise:

■ the shareholder has to have a prima facie case – frivolous or time-wasting claims will go nowhere;

■ the success of the company remains paramount – litigation will only go ahead if it's genuinely in the company's best interests;

■ the shareholder must be acting in good faith in the interests of the company as a whole;

■ the views of other shareholders will be taken into account, and an ordinary resolution in favour of the directors will trump all opposition;

■ a shareholder without a good case will be at risk on costs, its own and the company's.

The courts will not second guess a board decision taken in good faith that appeared reasonable at the time, whatever may have transpired subsequently.

These rules apply not just to a director's breach of the duties described in this book but also to a director's negligence and any other failure that may have been committed. There is no need to show that the director has benefited personally, and both present and past directors may be pursued. Shareholders can use the procedure to pre-empt an anticipated act or omission, as well as to claim for shortcomings in the past.

So what exactly is the procedure? A shareholder dissatisfied with a board's lack of action against an errant director must issue a claim in the name of the company and request the court's permission to take it forward. A successful shareholder will be allowed to pursue the claim (with the company footing the bill), but the court has a wide discretion to adjourn the case to gather evidence from the company itself. An unsuccessful shareholder risks paying the other parties' costs and an order restraining further action.

Crucially, permission to pursue a claim will only be granted if the court decides there is a prima facie case to answer. How will a court decide whether that prima facie case exists? The following are the key criteria:

■ Is it in the best interests of the company to pursue the matter through the courts; or does the shareholder have their own agenda/ulterior motives?

■ Would a director acting in accordance with the duty to promote the success of the company (see section 3) continue the claim?

If the decision is that such a hypothetical director would drop the claim, the case must be dismissed.

Other factors to be taken into account include: whether the shareholder is acting in good faith in bringing the claim (or just being vexatious); the views of other shareholders who have no personal interest in the claim; and whether the shareholder has other remedies available, such as a claim under a shareholders' agreement.

If the shareholders authorised the act complained of in advance, or they ratified it after the event, that's enough to stop the claim in its tracks.

Because the shareholder is claiming for the company's loss, not its own, it is irrelevant whether it has a million shares or just one, and whether it has owned those shares for decades or just days. Consequently, it's possible for a lobby group that objects to a company's environmental policies, say, to buy one share and launch a derivative claim against the directors for breach of duty. The fact that the harm complained of occurred before it became a shareholder is irrelevant. Such campaigners will nonetheless face an uphill task in convincing the court that they are acting in the company's best interests and not just pursuing their own narrow beliefs.

Dismissal

Whatever the circumstances, regardless of who is in the right and whether or not there has been a breach of duty, shareholders always have the right to remove a director by ordinary resolution. That right is enshrined in statute and cannot be taken away by a company's articles.

The director's employment rights will, however, be unaffected by the shareholder vote: the company will have to pay out for any notice period agreed under the director's service contract.

Shareholder ratification

Even where a director's breach of duty is clear, the shareholders can ratify it after the event by passing an ordinary resolution (that is, a simple majority vote – see Chapter 1, section 5). If the errant director is also a shareholder, they cannot vote in their own favour; neither can their family or others connected with them.

Excusing liability

A director in breach of a duty may also be relieved of any liability by the court if they can put forward a convincing argument that they acted honestly and reasonably in all the circumstances. This might happen where a director acted in good faith on the advice of a lawyer or other professional, but where the advice proved to be wrong.

Directors need not wait for proceedings against them before seeking the court's protection. They can bring their own action for a court order to exempt them from liability.

6. Directors and 'substantial' transactions

Section 4 detailed the requirements for a director to declare an interest in a contract with their company. If the transaction is above a certain value, the Companies Act 2006 also requires that the contract is approved by shareholders.

A director cannot enter into a contract to acquire anything of substance from the company, or to sell anything of substance to the company, unless shareholders have first approved the deal by passing an ordinary resolution, or the contract is conditional on getting that approval.

For this requirement to bite, the asset being bought or sold must have a value of more than £100,000 or 10 per cent of the company's net asset value as shown in its last accounts – where 10 per cent is equivalent to at least £5,000. (Note that although this requirement for shareholder approval is often referred to as applying to 'substantial property transactions' it does not relate exclusively to land and buildings. Any non-cash asset – for example, a trademark – can be included.)

This rule can be of particular relevance where a director is leaving a company, and part of the termination package includes the transfer of a company asset, perhaps a niche business in which the director has been working or a property they have been living in. But it does not apply to payments due under a director's service contract or to payments for loss of office.

The need for approval extends to transactions between a subsidiary and a director of the holding company – in which case, the shareholders of the holding company have to back the deal as well. It also applies to transactions between a company and a person who is connected with a director of the company (or its holding company) such as a family member or another company in which the director has at least a 20 per cent interest.

If requirements for approval are not met, the company has the option of setting the contract aside. In any event, without shareholder approval, the director is liable to the company for any profit they make on the contract and must indemnify the company for any loss it suffers.

7. Loans to directors

The Companies Act 2006 liberalised the law on a company lending money to its directors and, most importantly, dropped the criminal penalties if the rules were broken. Loans and similar transactions are now permitted if shareholders have given their approval. Where the loan is made by a subsidiary to a director of its parent company, the parent's shareholders must also give consent. In either case, a memorandum setting out the terms and purpose of the loan must be made available to the shareholders before the vote.

This is a useful relaxation for smaller companies, which often found themselves tripping over the previous ban on loans to directors; a company with a larger shareholder base is less likely to risk members' wrath trying to explain why such loans are necessary.

The requirements for shareholder approval and an explanatory memorandum do not apply in all cases. A company is free to:

■ Make loans to a director up to an aggregate total of £10,000.

■ Ignore the prohibition if it is in the business of lending money and it makes loans to directors on terms that are no more generous than might be offered to an outsider. (A director may be given a cheap mortgage provided the terms are no better than those offered to other employees, and the loan is for the director's only or main residence.)

■ Make loans to a director of a subsidiary, or of a fellow subsidiary, so long as the director is not also a director of the lending company.

■ Make loans to directors for the purpose of defending claims made against them or action brought by a regulator in connection with their position as directors. This applies to claims made by third parties or even by the company itself (though shareholders would be likely to question the company's decision to fund the defence to its own claim).

If the company in question is a plc, or is in the same group as a plc, the category of transactions requiring shareholder approval is widened and includes loans to people 'connected' with a director (for example, family members, a trustee for a director or their associated company), 'quasi-loans', credit transactions and related guarantees and security. Expenditure by a company on behalf of a director that is subsequently reimbursed may be caught, as may use of a company credit card for personal expenditure.

Note that even where a loan to a director is allowed without shareholder approval, it may still need to be disclosed in the company's accounts. In other words, it is not acceptable to keep loans to a director confidential.

8. Contracts with listed companies

If a company's shares are traded on the main market of the London Stock Exchange there is a further set of requirements before directors can contract with their own company.

Chapter 11 of the Listing Rules stipulates that where a transaction is proposed between a listed company or any of its subsidiaries and a 'related party', two things must happen: the company must send a circular to its shareholders explaining and valuing the transaction; and shareholders must formally approve the deal.

For these purposes, a related party includes:

■ a director of the company (including a shadow director);

■ a director of another company in the same group;

■ a holder of 10 per cent of the shares in the company or another company in the same group, or someone able to control 10 per cent of the votes attaching to those shares;

■ someone who is no longer such a director or shareholder but who was in the previous 12 months;

- someone who exercises a significant influence over the company;

- anyone connected with any of the above, such as immediate family, trustees or a related company.

Exemptions from the requirement for a circular and shareholder vote apply in a number of circumstances, including those listed below.

- The transaction has a revenue nature, rather than capital, and is 'in the ordinary course of business'. (Thus, shareholder approval would potentially be needed for a director buying a fixed asset from a listed company for £500,000, but not for the director to be paid an annual bonus of £500,000 if the bonus scheme could be said to be in the ordinary course of business.)

- The director or 10 per cent shareholder qualifies as a related party only by virtue of being a director or shareholder of an 'insignificant subsidiary' – that is, a subsidiary that has contributed less than 10 per cent of profits and represents less than 10 per cent of assets of the listed group in the past three financial years.

- The proposed transaction is a 'small transaction' – that is, one where various ratios detailed in the Listing Rules (for example, the amount to be paid under the transaction relative to the market capitalisation of the listed company) are no more than 0.25 per cent.

- The proposed transaction is outside the definition of small because one or more of the ratios detailed in the Listing Rules is above 0.25 per cent but all of them are still below five per cent. In this case, a company will be exempt from the normal requirements, but will have to obtain from an appropriate adviser confirmation that the terms of the proposed transaction are fair and reasonable so far as the shareholders are concerned. (Similar ratios apply to AIM companies. If any of them are five per cent or more, an AIM company must announce the transaction with the related party, disclosing certain specified details about it, and the board must confirm that, having consulted the company's nominated adviser, it considers the transaction to be fair and reasonable.)

9. Disclosure in the accounts of interests in contracts

Where a company or any of its subsidiaries enters into a transaction with a director of the company, the rules on disclosure, shareholder approval, loans and related parties may apply (see sections 4, 6, 7 and 8 above). Whether they do or not, information on such transactions may need to be included in the notes to the annual accounts.

Loans and quasi-loans must be set out, as must the directors' indemnities discussed in section 13 below. In addition, details are required of any transactions or arrangements where a director has a 'material interest'.

The obligation to disclose goes away if a director's transactions and arrangements in a financial year add up to no more than the higher of £1,000 or one per cent of the company's net asset value – subject to an overall limit of £5,000. Apart from that minimum level, what is 'material' is a question for the board to decide when putting the accounts together. If the board's decision is reasonable and made in good faith, it cannot be challenged.

This requirement to disclose can be a relevant factor in deciding whether or not to go ahead with a transaction.

10. Other statutory duties

A wide range of statutes imposes duties on directors, including those dealing with taxation, the environment and discrimination. We focus on health and safety in Chapter 9 and on competition law in section 12 below, but you do not have to stray beyond the Companies Act to find a variety of further duties. More than 200 involve offences directors can commit, with a variety of penalties applying to each. The majority are summary offences that are dealt with by a magistrate. Generally, the sanctions are fines and a criminal record for persistent offences, but in some cases the penalty will be imprisonment.

Most relate to administrative and compliance matters such as the proper maintenance and retention of books and records, and the preparation and lodging of documents and returns with the Registrar of Companies. A good company secretary can keep you out of trouble – see Chapter 3.

An example of a new tax-related duty came in the Finance Act of 2009: a company's senior accounting officer (usually the finance director) must certify annually that its accounting systems are adequate to ensure accurate tax reporting. If they are careless in giving such a certificate or deliberately wrong, the individual as well as the company is liable to penalties.

11. Liability for directors' reports, etc

It is worth looking in a little more detail at three areas where there is a mix of civil and criminal liability for what goes into a number of the reports directors are obliged to produce.

False or misleading statement in directors' reports

A director will be liable for any false or misleading statement in the annual directors' report and the directors' remuneration report or if they omit something from the reports that should have been included. But the director must have known the statement was wrong, or been reckless about it, or have been dishonest about leaving out the required information. (Recklessness requires a conscious disregard as to whether the information was right or wrong.)

Even if knowledge or recklessness can be proved, the director's liability is only to the company, not to any outside investor; and the company has to show that it has suffered a loss as a result.

False or misleading statement in periodic financial information

There is also liability for the financial information in a company's annual and half-year results and in the interim management statements that provide a quarterly update. This derives from the EU's Transparency Directive and applies only to listed companies in the United Kingdom (not those on AIM or PLUS).

But this is not a personal liability for a director. If an investor acquires shares in a listed company and later incurs a loss because of something untrue or misleading in the company's results, or because of the omission of a material fact, it is the company that will have to pay compensation. And the liability only crystallises if a director knew that the information was untrue or misleading, or was reckless on the point, or they left out the required information with the intention to deceive.

So dishonesty or recklessness is needed on the part of a director; honest mistakes should be excused.

Audit reports

It is a criminal offence for a director or company employee to give the auditors false or misleading information, or to fail to give them information they have asked for without delay. The first offence can lead to a two-year prison term; the second risks only a fine.

Directors are also under an obligation not to approve the company's accounts unless they are satisfied that they give a true and fair view of the financial position. In other words, they must not accept the opinion of the auditors automatically. They must separately ask themselves whether they believe the accounts are 'true and fair'.

12. Competition law

Companies can face civil penalties of up to 10 per cent of global turnover if they infringe competition law, and directors can be held personally liable for serious breaches of the EU and UK rules.

In the United Kingdom, an individual who participates in a cartel can be found guilty of a criminal offence (the so-called 'cartel offence'). It is an offence punishable by up to five years' imprisonment or an unlimited fine (or both) for an individual dishonestly to agree to enter into or implement certain anti-competitive agreements in the United Kingdom. These include direct or indirect price fixing, the limiting of production or supply, and market sharing or bid-rigging arrangements – ie the most serious 'hard core' breaches of competition law.

A director of a company that commits any breach of competition law can also be disqualified from acting as a director for up to 15 years on the basis that they were unfit to be involved in the management of a company.

What has to be proved for an individual to be held to be acting dishonestly? The court will apply a two-part test. First, was the individual acting dishonestly according to the standards of reasonable and honest people? Second, did they realise that what they were doing was dishonest by those standards?

The law also provides that a disqualification order can be issued against a company director if they knew, or ought to have known, that the company had breached EU or UK competition law. This sanction applies to any breach – not just the 'hard core' cartel infringements.

The Office of Fair Trading (OFT) wants to step up its enforcement of UK competition law and increase deterrence by using its powers more regularly to seek director disqualification orders, even where the director's involvement in the breach was indirect.

Directors, including the non-executives, are not expected to be experts on competition law, but they need to appreciate that competition law compliance is a crucial matter for their companies. The OFT and other regulators expect every director to know that price-fixing, market sharing and bid-rigging agreements are unlawful and that they can't simply turn a blind eye to suspicious activity within the company. Signing off an expenses claim for an unlawful meeting could be enough for a director to be caught. The OFT will, however, take into account any actions taken by such a director to create a compliance culture and to avoid breaches of competition law.

13. Indemnity and insurance protection

To what extent can a company protect its directors from some of the liabilities outlined in this chapter, including any legal costs that might be involved? There are two possible options:

■ giving directors an exemption from any liability to the company and an indemnity against liability to third parties;

■ taking out and paying for insurance against any liability incurred by the directors.

The giving of exemptions is banned by the Companies Act, and indemnities are restricted; insurance policies need to be carefully read to ensure they cover the desired risks.

Indemnities

A company can indemnify its directors against personal liability so long as the indemnity does not cover:

■ liability to the company in cases where the company sues the director – only liability to third parties can be the subject of an indemnity;

■ liability for fines for criminal conduct or fines imposed by a regulator such as the Financial Services Authority (FSA);

■ other liabilities (such as legal costs) in criminal cases where the director is convicted, or in civil cases brought by the company where the final judgment goes against the director.

So a company can give an indemnity that will commit it to paying any or all of the following:

■ directors' legal costs in civil claims brought by a third party, even if the judgment goes against them;

■ the costs of any damages or other award made against directors if they lose civil claims brought against them by a third party;

■ directors' legal costs if they are acquitted in criminal proceedings;

■ directors' costs in fighting civil proceedings brought by the FSA (for example, for a breach of the Listing Rules).

A company's articles will usually permit the giving of these indemnities.

But it is a mistake to think an indemnity in the articles is all that is required. A director cannot enforce an indemnity through the articles alone. A separate commitment from the company is needed in a service contract or other document.

The general restrictions on a company making loans to its directors (see section 7) do not prevent a company from funding a director's ongoing defence costs in either civil or criminal proceedings, provided that the terms on which the funding is advanced require the director to repay the money if they are convicted or final judgment is given against them. This applies even when it is the company itself that is suing the director.

Any indemnities given to directors have to be disclosed each year in the directors' report that accompanies the audited accounts and their terms have to be available to shareholders at all times. These rules apply also where one company in a group indemnifies the directors of another.

Whether companies should take full advantage of this ability to give indemnities is not a straightforward question. Given the growing burden of their responsibilities and liabilities, and a fear that litigation is on the increase, directors will be keen to have the benefit of every permissible form of protection. But in setting its policy, a board will need to decide whether it believes it is right to give an indemnity in every case – for example, where a director has clearly acted dishonestly or beyond their authority. If money is advanced to a director to meet defence costs in actions brought by the company, it will be necessary to:

■ explain the decision carefully to shareholders, who may wonder why the company appears to be helping someone it believes did it harm;

■ consider how the costs are going to be recouped from the director if the company wins.

Insurance

A company is allowed to take out and pay for insurance to cover liabilities incurred by its directors. Indeed, doing so can be considered part of best practice. The UK Corporate Governance Code, whose guidelines are followed by a wide range of organisations (see Chapter 4), states that: 'The company should arrange appropriate insurance cover in respect of legal action against its directors'.

The question of insurance needs to be looked at in the context of any indemnities given by the company, as discussed above. If the company decides to insure, it may want to take out cover in respect of those risks it cannot indemnify its directors against – or chooses not to do so. The company may also want to insure itself for liabilities where it has given an indemnity to its directors.

Whatever the company decides to do, it is important for the board as a whole, and for individual directors, to appreciate that there is no standard insurance policy that answers all needs. The exact terms of a policy will be interpreted restrictively, and so all concerned must have a clear understanding of what is covered and what is not. A director is taking a big risk if they simply assume that a directors' and officers' (D&O) insurance policy is in place and will cover them without taking the time to establish exactly what protection it affords.

A new director should at least establish that the insurer is aware of their appointment and that they will be covered by the policy. And both new and existing directors need to satisfy themselves on the terms of the policy. Some of the key points to consider are listed in the following box.

Like a company indemnity, insurance will not provide a complete safeguard for a director against personal liability. It is only part of the answer. Clarification from the company secretary and, if necessary, from insurance brokers and legal advisers, is advisable where there is any doubt.

Directors' and Officers' Insurance Policies: Questions to Ask

■ Does the policy cover both past and present directors so that a director remains covered once they leave the company for actions taken during the period of appointment? A claim may not arise for some time after the director has stepped down.

■ Who is covered? A policy will usually protect those who sit on the main board and those who are also directors of subsidiary companies. It will not necessarily extend to those who are nominated to be directors of joint venture companies or companies in which the holding company has only a minority stake.

■ How does the policy deal with newly acquired businesses? Does cover only start from the date of acquisition, excluding liability for acts committed before then?

■ What risks are covered? Few cases go all the way to judgment; most are settled out of court. It is important, therefore, to find out whether claims for sums agreed in out-of-court settlements can be made.

- What are the exclusions? Invariably, the policy will not cover fraud, deliberate dishonesty and illegal acts; nor will fines and penalties imposed by the criminal courts and by regulators such as the FSA be included.

- What legal costs and expenses are covered? Will they be paid on an interim basis during the course of a case? Are they recoverable if the director loses? Legal costs for an appeal against a criminal conviction will usually be excluded – the insurer will not pay for you to fight your case all the way to the Supreme Court.

- Will advisers' costs (both legal and accountancy) also be paid for government and FSA investigations?

- Will the policy cover claims made outside the United Kingdom? Some jurisdictions may be excluded. For example, a director of a company with operations or subsidiaries in North America may not be covered for actions originating there.

- What about claims made against directors by their own company? Some policies will exclude liability for a claim made by one party against another insured under the same policy. (The precise wording of the policy will be crucial here; establishing what is included and what is not will require careful checking.)

- What are the monetary limits on claims? Many companies are woefully under-insured. A company and its directors could effectively be left uninsured if one or two big claims in the same year have used up the sum insured. The more people insured under the policy, the greater the risk of this happening.

- What about 'excesses' or 'deductibles'? Different risks may carry different excesses. Where they apply, are they payable by the company or by the director?

3

The Company Secretary

The job of the company secretary has changed over the years, both in perception and in fact. As long ago as 1971 the influential judge Lord Denning commented that the secretary:

> is an officer of the company with extensive duties and responsibilities ... He is no longer a mere clerk.

That process has accelerated more recently, with the post coming to play a key role in the governance of many companies (see section 3 below).

1. The role

Until 6 April 2008 all UK companies, public or private, needed to have a company secretary. The paradox is that then, as now, there was no job description for the company secretary in companies legislation. As a result, many small private companies filled the post by giving it to one of the directors. A company with only one director could not double up the role, so a spouse or employee was often press-ganged into service.

Private company

The implementation of the Companies Act 2006 means that private companies can now choose whether to have a company secretary or not. They are under no statutory requirement to fill the role. (They may, though, have to change their articles before dispensing with the job: the Act does not overrule the articles on the point.)

Very small private companies where there is no real need for the role are the most obvious beneficiaries of the new rule. But it's been good news for others, too.

In many private companies there remains an administrative job to be done, whether a company secretary is formally appointed to do it or not. There are still returns to be filed with Companies House, registers to be kept up to date, paperwork to be processed. The difference is that there is now no requirement for the person doing the job to be registered at Companies House as secretary, or to file new particulars when the secretary changes. In large corporate groups, with a hundred or more subsidiaries, that is a worthwhile benefit.

Where there is no company secretary, and no deputy or assistant, the Companies Act says that anything required to be done by the secretary can instead be done by someone authorised by the board. Similarly, anything to be done to the secretary, such as the service of a notice, can be done to anyone authorised by the directors for that purpose.

Public company

A public company, by contrast, must have a secretary. Not only that, the person doing the job must have some qualification for the post. The Companies Act says:

■ the directors of a public company have a duty to take all reasonable steps to ensure that the secretary of the company is a person who 'appears to them to have the requisite knowledge and experience to discharge the functions of secretary of the company';

■ the secretary must also:

 – have been secretary of a public company for at least three of the five years preceding the appointment;

 – be a member of the Institute of Chartered Accountants in England and Wales (or the Scottish or Irish equivalent), or of the Association of Chartered Certified Accountants, the Chartered Institute of Management Accountants or the Chartered Institute of Public Finance and Accountancy;

- be a member of the Institute of Chartered Secretaries and Administrators;

- be a barrister, advocate or solicitor called or admitted in the UK; or

- be a person who, by virtue of holding or having held any other position or being a member of any other body, appears to the directors to be capable of discharging the functions of secretary of the company.

That last alternative 'qualification' is rather a catch-all, allowing the appointment of anyone else the board favours, but it at least makes the point that the directors need to be able to justify their selection on the basis of the candidate's past experience.

The job will often be combined with other roles in the company. The general counsel or in-house lawyer may double up as secretary, giving directors the benefit of on-the-spot legal advice as they make their decisions. (The company secretary always attends board meetings.) A finance director filling the post may be a less desirable option, particularly when a degree of independence is required (see section 3 on governance, page 61). In some cases, a director may nominally act as company secretary, but an assistant or deputy secretary will do the day-to-day work.

Corporate secretaries

A company secretary does not have to be an individual but can instead be another company or a partnership. Indeed, many lawyers and accountants provide company secretarial services to their clients by means of a corporate secretary. A company cannot be a member of any of the organisations listed above as qualifying bodies for a public company secretary, so reliance has to be placed on the final category of holding 'any other position'. Alternatively, the post may be filled nominally by a qualified individual at the plc, but with most of the work outsourced to the corporate body.

ICSA

The Institute of Chartered Secretaries and Administrators (ICSA), the membership body for company secretaries, awards the qualification Chartered Secretary through a programme that is now international in its scope. ICSA also liaises with government on questions of practice and law and produces useful publications and guidance notes, many of which are available on its website for free.

2. Duties

As noted above, there is no easily accessible job description for a company secretary. There are certain duties dotted around the Companies Act that are core to the role of most holders of the office, but there are other responsibilities often added to the post, such as property management, pensions administration, the operation of share and other incentive schemes, and maintaining adequate insurance cover. In this section we concentrate on some of the core duties and the rules and regulations that a company secretary will commonly need to apply.

These duties have in the past been divided into those owed to the board, to the company and to shareholders. A fourth category can be added today to include those responsibilities imposed by regulators that are commonly discharged by the secretary.

The board

The secretary attends all board meetings and is directly answerable to the board (see also the next section on governance). Meetings of the directors will be convened by the secretary in conjunction with the chairman, and one of the secretary's prime functions will be to produce minutes of a board meeting. (The same goes for committees of the board.) Indeed, it is a requirement of the Companies Act that minutes of all meetings of directors are produced and kept for at least 10 years – failure to do so is an offence punishable by a fine.

The minutes should, of course, be an accurate record of the meeting. They should state the reasons for a decision either explicitly or by reference to an accompanying board paper – particularly where the resulting benefit for the company may not be obvious. Should any decision of the board be challenged at a later date, the minutes and board papers will be a valuable record of the board's thinking at the time (see the box in Chapter 2 on decision taking and record keeping, pages 29–30).

Problems can arise where there is disagreement as to what was said at a meeting or what decision was arrived at. Minutes of one meeting should be circulated before they are tabled for approval at the next. If any disagreements cannot be resolved at that stage, the majority view should prevail. Where the approved minutes do not record the dissenting minority's views to their satisfaction, the remedy is for them to write to the chairman setting out their position and to circulate copies to all board members. That way, they have a written contemporaneous record of what they said as an alternative to the official minutes.

The company

Another core task for the secretary is the maintenance of the statutory registers. These include those listed below.

■ The share register, which is the definitive record of who the company's shareholders are, who can vote and to whom dividends are paid. Transfers of shares need to be entered in the register and dealt with according to the company's articles. Most companies with a share register of any size will contract out this work to professional registrars, but see the box on page 57 on access to shareholders' addresses.

■ The registers of directors and secretaries that record the personal details of the company's office holders and reflect the information filed at Companies House. See the box on page 58 on disclosure of the home addresses of both directors and secretaries.

■ The register of charges in which details of all mortgages and other charges granted by the company to its lenders and other parties must be recorded.

There are many returns that a company needs to make to Companies House to update the information held on the public record – changes to the board, share issues, the passing of certain shareholder resolutions and the annual return, which is a snapshot of the company at a particular date in the year, recording details of the directors, the issued share capital and the current shareholders.

The secretary will also often be the person responsible for ensuring the company's name and other details appear where they should on business stationery and at any premises where the company carries on business – see the box on page 59.

The shareholders

The secretary will also look after communications with shareholders. This will include sending them the Report and Accounts each year, and convening shareholder meetings – the annual general meeting for a public company and for a private company that chooses to continue with an AGM, and other general meetings where shareholder approval is needed (see Chapter 1, section 5). Provided you have the right processes in place, all these communications can now be made electronically – see the box on page 60.

The share register will only show the names of the holders of the legal title in the company's shares. They may be nominees or trustees for others who have the beneficial or economic interest in the shares, and so the register will not be a true reflection of who really owns the company.

Where shares in a UK company are traded on the main list of the London Stock Exchange or on AIM, anyone with an interest in three per cent or more of the voting rights must notify the company, and the company in turn must notify the market. That obligation applies when the interest is first acquired and when it increases or decreases. (The rules differ for overseas companies on the main list or AIM.)

A public company can require disclosure of share interests, not just from shareholders as to their underlying beneficial owners, but also from third parties whom it suspects of having an interest at any time in the previous three years. This power is frequently exercised by companies facing a takeover or when they are nervous about possible stake-building by a predator, and it will commonly be the secretary's job to keep on top of these changes in legal and beneficial ownership. Registrars have sophisticated systems that will help in the process.

The regulators

A listed company must comply with the FSA's Listing Rules and the Disclosure and Transparency Rules (DTRs). (AIM companies face many of the same obligations.) These comprise a myriad of regulations; the main ones for a company secretary are listed below.

- DTR2, which requires the prompt disclosure of 'inside information' – see Chapter 5, section 1. The secretary will usually manage that disclosure process and provide the first advice to the board as to whether an announcement to the market is necessary.

- The Model Code in Chapter 9 of the Listing Rules, which regulates when directors and other 'persons discharging managerial responsibilities' (PDMRs) can and cannot deal in the company's shares – see Chapter 5, section 5. The secretary will often be designated as the person who gives or refuses permission to deal.

- DTR3, which applies once a director or other PDMR has dealt in the company's shares and requires details of the dealing to be disclosed to the market within four business days.

Authority and execution of documents

The secretary is an officer of the company. What authority does that confer on him or her? In a 1971 case, a company secretary hired cars in the name of the company that were in fact for his own private use. The car hire business sued the company when it refused to pay, and won. It was entitled to rely on the secretary's ostensible authority, as the company's chief administrative officer. The Court of Appeal ruled that the secretary:

regularly makes representations on behalf of the company and enters into contracts on its behalf which come within the day-to-day running of the company's business, so much so that he may be regarded as held out as having authority to do such things on behalf of the company. He is certainly entitled to sign contracts connected with the administrative side of a company's affairs, such as employing staff, and ordering cars, and so forth.

As an employee of the company, a secretary will in any event often have actual authority delegated by the board to enter into commercial contracts on behalf of the company. Authority for the secretary to commit the company may also be implied by a regular course of dealing over time.

Execution of formal documents, such as property deeds or mortgage documents, used to need the signatures of two directors, or of one director and the secretary. The removal of the requirement for private companies to have a company secretary, however, forced a change in the rules. Since April 2008, any company, public or private, has been able to execute a document in one of four ways:

■ by the signature of a single director witnessed by a second person (who need not be a director or connected in any way with the company);

■ by applying the company's common seal to the document (if it has one), witnessed by two directors or by a director and the secretary;

■ by the signature of two directors;

■ by the signature of a director and the secretary.

A word of warning: allowing one director to sign on behalf of a company may be administratively convenient, but it can leave an individual exposed to making major decisions on their own that will bind the company. Two heads can be better than one, so best practice may be for internal company policy to insist on two signatures.

Access to Shareholders' Addresses

Before the Companies Act 2006, a company's share register was open to inspection by all: shareholders could see it for free; everyone else had to pay a charge, but only a modest one. What's more, copies had to be supplied on request.

This ready access, however, was open to abuse – not only by direct marketing companies after a cheap mailing list, but also by those with more sinister motives. To protect shareholders, the government introduced a 'proper purpose' test. What exactly that means is not defined in the legislation and is left to the courts to decide. Shareholders wanting to communicate with each other, or a bidder wanting shareholder information as a prelude to a takeover, are likely to be 'proper'; junk mailers and those pursuing an unlawful purpose are not.

The person wanting to inspect the register or receive a copy of it (whether they are a shareholder or not) must first supply the company with:

■ their name and address (if an organisation, the name and address of an individual responsible for making the request is also needed);

■ the purpose for which the information is to be used;

■ whether the information is to be disclosed to any other person and if so, the same details as above for that person.

It is a criminal offence for a person to supply false, misleading or deceptive information in such a request, or to supply information from the share register to a person who hasn't been named.

Having received a request, the company has five working days either to comply or, if it wishes to refuse, to apply to the court. The court can either uphold the request for access, in which event the company must supply the information immediately, or direct the company to deny it.

Disclosure of Home Addresses of Directors and Secretaries

Until October 2009, the home addresses of directors and secretaries were available for all to see at Companies House. If an individual could show that they were at serious risk of violence or intimidation, a confidentiality order could be applied for and, if granted, their private address would then be kept from public view. This was of most obvious use to those directors under threat from animal rights activists.

Since October 2009, only service addresses, which may be the company's registered office or any other business address, have had to appear on the public record. Directors still have to give a home address to their company on appointment, and the company still has to pass that address on to Companies House, but it's now kept confidential, with no right of access for the general public. (Secretaries need only give a service address.)

This confidentiality is not absolute: two groups continue to have access to home addresses: public authorities such as the police, HM Revenue & Customs and the FSA; and credit reference agencies (because the credit worthiness of directors may affect their companies' access to bank lending). The latter can still be denied access if a director believes that they, and anyone who lives with them, is at serious risk of violence or intimidation; evidence of police involvement and quoting a police incident number will help any application for confidentiality.

The big drawback with these rules is that home addresses already at Companies House before 1 October 2009 continue to be available. They will not be removed unless you can show you're at serious risk of violence or intimidation because of the activities of the company on whose board you sit. Even then, only addresses back to 1 January 2003 will be removed (the technical problems of removing older addresses are too great).

If you continue to live at an address given to Companies House before 2003, there is nothing you can do to keep it confidential. The only solution is to move.

Company Details on Stationery and at Business Premises

A company is legally required to publicise its name, address and certain other details on business stationery and to display its name at its business premises. The rules are listed below.

■ **Business letters and order forms** must include in legible characters a company's:

- full name;

- registered number;

- registered office address;

- the part of the UK where the company is registered.

If the company is exempt from using the word 'limited' in its name, it also needs to state that it is a limited company. If a business letter names a director of the company (other than in the text or as a signatory), all directors must be named.

■ **All other business stationery** must disclose the company's full name in a form that is capable of being read with the naked eye. This includes sales literature, cheques and all correspondence.

■ **E-mails** – the rules for business letters, order forms and other business stationery apply whether in hard or soft copy form. Companies therefore need to ensure that a standard footer containing the requisite details is added at the end of all e-mails. Where several companies operate from the same e-mail address, the footer needs to include details for all the companies on whose behalf the e-mail might be sent.

■ A company's **website** must carry the same details as its business letters and order forms. Where a group of companies shares a website, the details for all companies that make use of the site and are identified on it need to appear.

■ **Business premises** – a company is required to display its full name at its registered office and at any location at which it keeps company records available for inspection. In addition, the name must also be on show at any other site where the company carries on business. That will include any premises from which the company operates, even if that operation is small scale or infrequent. The name needs to be displayed in such a way that it can be easily seen by a visitor. Companies whose activities put their directors at serious risk of violence or intimidation can be exempt from these requirements.

Electronic Communication with Shareholders

All companies can communicate with their shareholders electronically rather than by sending hard copies through the post, but only if their articles allow them to do so, or a shareholder resolution is passed to that effect.

A company can send documents by e-mail where the recipient has agreed and given an address.

A further provision is useful for companies with large shareholder lists – they can send documents and supply information to shareholders by posting them on a company website, so long as:

■ the shareholders have passed a resolution to permit this or the articles allow for it;

■ every shareholder has been asked to agree to receipt of documents via the website and has consented – or failed to object – within 28 days.

Even once that process has been gone through, the company still has to notify shareholders each time a document or information appears on the website and, unless e-mail addresses have been supplied, that notice needs to be by hard copy letter.

Documents and notices can be supplied to a company in electronic form by a shareholder or third party where the company is in agreement – ie where it has given an e-mail address on a related document.

3. Governance

The growing importance placed on corporate governance has enhanced the role of the company secretary. The holder of the post is now seen in many respects as the guardian of a company's governance and an independent adviser to the board.

The UK Corporate Governance Code (see Chapter 4) makes this point:

The company secretary should be responsible for advising the board through the chairman on all governance matters.

The secretary thus has a responsibility to all directors, but, for practical reasons, the chairman needs to retain some control.

The Code sees the secretary as a resource for the whole board:

All directors should have access to the advice and services of the company secretary, who is responsible to the board for ensuring that board procedures are complied with.

And the administrative role is crucial:

Under the direction of the chairman, the company secretary's responsibilities include ensuring good information flows within the board and its committees and between senior management and non-executive directors, as well as facilitating induction and assisting with professional development as required.

Not only is the secretary in many ways a chief of staff to the chairman in running an efficient and effective board, but there is also a relationship with each director who might seek the independent view of the secretary on an area of potential dispute or controversy. (This is why it can be problematic if an executive director is also the company secretary.)

Non-executives can in particular look to the secretarial team for help and guidance in their role and to understand fully proposals coming before the board. If they want to seek independent advice outside the company (as encouraged by the Code), that can often be achieved through the company secretary.

Induction of new directors was an area highlighted by the 2009 Walker Report as a means of improving the effectiveness of non-executive directors, who might come to their post with little or no knowledge of the workings of the company and its board, and possibly little experience of its business sector. The secretary has a key role in designing and implementing an induction process that quickly and efficiently gives directors the knowledge they need to play a full part in the boardroom.

This semi-independent role enjoyed by the secretary is bolstered by the Code requirement that their appointment or removal be a matter for the board as a whole. No one director, even the chairman, should be in a position to hire or fire the secretary.

4. Liabilities

A company secretary may not be a director, but they will often be liable for breach of duty in the same way as board members. The code of directors' duties, set out in the Companies Act, is not expressed as applying to the secretary, but, as an officer of the company, the duty to promote the company's success should apply in equal measure, as should the obligations to avoid a conflict of interest and to exercise independent judgment. (Note that these duties are owed to the company and not directly to shareholders.)

As discussed above, the secretary has many administrative responsibilities, including filing returns at Companies House and ensuring compliance with the Companies Act. Numerous sections in the Act provide that, where there is a failure to file or comply, 'an offence is committed by every officer of the company who is in default'. If the secretary is the person with prime responsibility for the task, they will be the person in default and liable to the fine.

4

Corporate Governance

This chapter concentrates on the main terms of the Financial Reporting Council's (FRC's) UK Corporate Governance Code (formerly known as the Combined Code) and on their implications for directors. The latest edition of the Code, incorporating some of the recommendations of the 2009 Walker Report (see the box on page 64) can be found on the FRC's website.

1. The development of the UK Corporate Governance Code

Governance is a word that barely existed 30 years ago. Now it is in common use not just in companies but also in charities, universities, local authorities and National Health Trusts. It has become a shorthand for the way an organisation is run, with particular emphasis on its accountability, integrity and risk management.

The 'revolution' started in the early 1990s with the groundbreaking report from Sir Adrian Cadbury on the financial aspects of corporate governance, which produced a two-page code of best practice. Aimed at listed companies and looking especially at standards of corporate behaviour and ethics, the 'Cadbury Code' was gradually adopted by the City and the Stock Exchange as a benchmark of good boardroom practice and, in 1998, after further reports from two more City grandees, it evolved into the Combined Code on Corporate Governance.

Continuing shareholder disquiet over perceived shortcomings in corporate structures and their ability to respond to poor performance, as well as threats of legislation if the corporate sector failed to put its house in order, brought more reviews of corporate governance – and more revisions to the Code. By 2003, sections had been added on remuneration, risk management, internal control and audit committees.

In 2008, the banking crisis and the effective nationalisation of several UK banks led the government to ask Sir David Walker to look specifically at corporate governance in UK banks and other large financial institutions (see the box below). That was closely followed by a more general review of the Code by the FRC, the body established by government with the task, among other things, of overseeing the operation of the Code. A new version duly came out, this time with a new title – the UK Corporate Governance Code. It applies to company accounting periods beginning on or after 29 June 2010.

Is all this attention on governance good for business, in the hard, commercial sense? Views differ. Several surveys have claimed that companies with better corporate governance are more profitable; sceptics have countered that it is only the more successful companies that can afford the time and effort to make sure they follow best practice. There is no doubt, however, that the demand of shareholders and other stakeholders for good governance is strong and continuing. Investors, regulators, government and assorted pressure groups are all increasingly likely to condemn a business that fails to follow the 'rules'. The business case for good corporate governance is, therefore, not difficult to build.

The Walker Report

With a career spanning the Treasury, the Bank of England, a City regulator and UK and US banks, Sir David Walker was perhaps a natural choice to review corporate governance in the light of the 2008 banking crisis. The question he sought to answer was this: if different banks were operating in the same areas and under the same regulators, why did some fail and some survive – what differences in their governance led to such different results?

More specifically, Walker was asked to look at:

■ how to improve risk management at board level;

■ whether incentive and bonus schemes encourage risk taking;

■ the right balance of skills, experience and independence on a board of directors;

■ the role of institutional shareholders in talking to and monitoring boards of directors.

The 2009 Walker Report made 39 recommendations for better governance. It's important to remember that they were aimed at banks, large insurance companies and other financial institutions. Some are relevant for companies in other sectors and therefore feature in the FRC's UK Corporate Governance Code from June 2010; others will act as examples of best practice in particular cases.

2. The reach of the Code

The FRC may be the custodian of the Code but compliance is a matter for the Listing Rules. Produced by the Financial Services Authority, these Rules regulate all companies (UK and overseas) with a premium listing on the London Stock Exchange.

The Code does not apply to:

■ companies whose shares are traded on AIM or other markets not covered by the Listing Rules (see the box on page 66 for a discussion on governance in AIM companies);

■ a listed company with a standard listing on the London Stock Exchange (previously known as a 'secondary' listing and confined to overseas companies, but now available to UK corporates as well).

There is, though, nothing to stop such companies complying with the Code if they choose to do so. Shareholder pressure, or simply a wish to conform with 'best practice', may lead many 'exempt' companies to follow some or all of the Code's recommendations. Most of the Code's principles, if not all the detailed provisions, provide a sound basis for the governance of many companies.

Indeed, the Code's reach has come to extend beyond its immediate 'target group' – what follows in this chapter may be of help to directors, trustees, governors and council members in many disparate organisations. The Code has been the impetus for the development of a more formalised approach to governance in other sectors. Higher education institutions have produced much useful material on governance; public sector bodies have guidance from the Independent Commission on Good Governance in Public Services. And mutual life companies are expected to follow guidelines on governance produced in the wake of the Equitable Life inquiry.

AIM Companies and Governance

The UK Corporate Governance Code does not apply to AIM companies, and there is no equivalent set of guidelines in the AIM Rules. One reason for this is that AIM is a less regulated market, attracting companies from around the world by its 'light touch' regime. Given this absence of regulation, the safeguard for shareholders is the broker or sponsor that acts as the company's nominated adviser or 'nomad'.

The nomad is in many ways the conscience of the company, checking, cautioning and advising the company on compliance with the rules and good practice. Two obligations highlight this role:

■ when a company floats on AIM, the nomad should consider with the directors 'the adoption of appropriate corporate governance measures';

■ the nomad needs to be satisfied that the company has in place 'sufficient systems, procedures and controls' to comply with the AIM Rules.

That is the limit of the governance regulation on AIM. And with many AIM companies based overseas, sometimes with large family or founder shareholdings, there is great flexibility for controls that fit the local circumstances.

For those who nonetheless want a ready-made code, there is a set of guidelines produced for AIM companies by the Quoted Companies Alliance (available from the QCA – see www.qcanet. co.uk for details and cost). These do not have a comply or explain format (see section 4, page 67), but rather are a set of minimum standards to be followed in their entirety.

Whether you adopt the basic rules from the QCA or favour compliance with the relevant bits of the Code, best practice suggests you should describe your governance systems each year in the company's annual Directors' Report.

---

3. The Code and the annual report

The Code is divided into 'main principles', 'supporting principles' and 'provisions'. The main principles are general statements of corporate life, which, at times, come close to motherhood and apple pie in their level of general acceptability. The first, for example, states: 'Every company should be headed by an effective board, which is collectively responsible for the long-term success of the company.' Supporting principles expand on the main principles and give more guidance. But it is the Code's provisions that state the detailed requirements necessary, in the view of the Code's authors, to make sure the principles are upheld.

The Listing Rules seek to give the principles and provisions some force by placing two requirements on companies with a premium listing.

■ The annual report and accounts must contain a statement explaining how the company has applied the main principles. (It's taken for granted that those principles are accepted; the only room for debate is over how they are applied.)

■ The report and accounts must state whether the company has complied with the provisions throughout the year covered by the report. If the company has not complied with all of the provisions, or if it has complied with them for only part of the year, the departures must be listed and reasons for the non-compliance given.

4. The comply or explain rule

This brings us to a key feature of the UK Corporate Governance Code, copied to an extent by other codes derived from it: its regime of 'comply or explain'. Listed companies must comply with the Code's detailed provisions or explain why they do not. Ignoring the Code is not an option; but if you have good reason to deviate from its terms, you may do so and leave it up to your shareholders to decide whether your reason is good enough.

So non-compliance with a term of the Code is not a breach; failure to explain is. If you can talk to shareholders and demonstrate that departures from the Code's provisions are consistent with its principles and in the company's best interests, then non-compliance is unlikely to become a big issue.

Shareholders have no specific sanction if they disapprove of what you are doing, short of registering a protest vote against the directors' remuneration report if the debate is over boardroom pay, or voting one or more directors off the board – a somewhat extreme step. What they can do, though, is apply pressure with the aim of persuading the board to change its mind.

As the case of the supermarket chain Morrisons shows, this can be most effective at those junctures when a company needs the support of its shareholders. (See box on page 68.)

If the shareholders are not big enough or well organised enough to exert pressure or if they are unwilling to take the opportunities they have to do so, then the board can decide how much it complies. The key point is that the Code and its provisions are not compulsory; they are there for guidance and represent best practice.

Morrisons: How Shareholders Can Change Governance

Some years ago, the supermarket chain Morrisons seemed unencumbered by corporate governance principles. The company, led by the septuagenarian Sir Ken Morrison as full-time executive chairman, had no non-executive directors, no audit or remuneration committees and no shame in explaining that it did not think these were necessary. It was a FTSE 100 company and very much in the public eye. Institutional shareholders might not have liked its public defiance of generally accepted principles, but Morrisons was successful, and there was little they could do about it.

Things began to change after Sir Ken decided to bid for rival chain Safeway in 2003. The chairman needed to raise money for the bid from shareholders, and one of the conditions they imposed was that he should at least appoint two non-executive directors. Over a year later and just before the AGM, two new non-executives duly appeared (though one resigned 10 months later). One institutional shareholder group commented, recognising the uphill task they still faced: 'We welcome this step towards better corporate governance and hope to see formal board committees established in due course.'

Integration of the Safeway stores did not go smoothly, profit warnings followed and the company acknowledged failures in its internal controls, all of which gave shareholders the opportunity to argue that its governance wasn't working. Step by step, Morrisons came to have a full complement of board committees, a majority of non-executives on the board and to separate the roles of chairman and chief executive.

---

5. The role of the board

The Code sets out its own view of the role of the board. This can be summarised as:

■ providing entrepreneurial leadership;

- setting strategy;
- ensuring the human and financial resources are available to achieve objectives;
- reviewing management performance;
- setting the company's values and standards;
- ensuring that obligations to shareholders and other stakeholders are understood and met.

The Code recognises that there are some issues that can only be decided by the board. It states that: 'there should be a formal schedule of matters specifically reserved for its decision' and that the annual report should include a 'high-level statement of which types of decisions are to be taken by the board and which are to be delegated to management'. Guidance on drawing up a schedule of matters reserved for the board is available from the Institute of Chartered Secretaries and Administrators (ICSA) and from *The Effective Board*, sister publication to this book.

6. The chairman

The chairman leads the board, sets its agenda and ensures it is an effective working group at the head of the company. He must promote a culture of openness and debate and is responsible for effective communication with shareholders (but note the role of the senior independent director as well – see section 10, below). And he must ensure that all board members receive accurate, timely and clear information.

The Code says the roles of chairman and chief executive should not be held by the same person:

> There should be a clear division of responsibilities at the head of the company between the running of the board and the executive responsibility for the running of the company's business. No one individual should have unfettered powers of decision – main principle A.2.

The chairman may not always be a part-time non-executive: many are full time and describe themselves as executive chairman, but the roles of chairman and CEO are at least distinct. In addition to the responsibilities described above, the chairman ensures there is a good working relationship between the executive and non-executive directors and sufficient time to discuss strategic issues.

By contrast, the chief executive has responsibility for the day-to-day management of the company and putting into effect the decisions and policies of the board.

Any big public company combining the roles of chairman and CEO will have to persuade shareholders that the right checks and balances are in place. (See the box on Marks & Spencer below).

Equally to be frowned upon, according to the Code, is the previously widespread practice of a chief executive stepping up to become chairman of the same company. Those against the practice argue that a new chief executive is going to have a next to impossible job if his predecessor stays as chairman, constantly looking over his shoulder and perhaps disagreeing with any departure from past policies. Those in favour sing the praises of a chairman who may have years of experience with the company, still has much to offer and who is quite capable of establishing a good working relationship with a new CEO.

The Code does concede that in exceptional cases the rule may be broken. Any board in breach should consult major shareholders in advance and set out its reasons for the appointment, both at the time and in the next annual report. Banks, in particular, have argued that only the incumbent CEO has the knowledge and experience of a large, multinational group's operations to fulfil the chairman's role.

This view received some indirect backing from the Walker Report, which argued for a greater emphasis on relevant industry experience among non-executive directors. And much play was made of the fact that of the three UK banks that failed in 2007–2008, RBS, HBOS and Northern Rock, none had a chairman with a banking background. In contrast, the chairmen of HSBC and Standard Chartered, which emerged relatively unscathed from the banking crisis, were lifetime bankers (and both had stepped up from the chief executive role).

How Marks & Spencer Got Its Way

Marks & Spencer is a rare case of a major company where the roles of chairman and chief executive have been combined.

In 2008, the chief executive, Sir Stuart Rose, was handed the chairman's job as well – in contravention of principle A.2. Shareholders muttered that this was contrary to the Code, but the company stressed that the roles would be split again when Sir Stuart retired in 2011. In the meantime, the new chairman's dominance would be counterbalanced by the senior independent director, who was given special responsibility for governance issues.

When a resolution was tabled at the July 2009 AGM calling for the early appointment of an independent chairman, it received an unusually high level of support, from 38 per cent of voting shareholders, but 62 per cent backed the board, and Sir Stuart remained in place. Despite that, a new chief executive joined in early 2010, and the roles were once again separated.

7. The role of the non-executive director

The Code clearly gives a strong role to the non-executives. Their job description includes:

■ constructive challenge and help in developing proposals on strategy;

■ scrutiny of management's performance in meeting agreed goals and objectives and the monitoring of performance reports;

■ satisfying themselves on the integrity of financial information and that controls and risk management systems are robust and defensible;

■ determining appropriate levels of remuneration for executive directors;

■ appointing and removing executive directors, and succession planning.

The Walker Report has re-emphasised the constructive challenge part of the job, in the light of the perceived quiescence of bank directors faced by a dominant chief executive. And the role of the non-executives in setting pay in banks has been widened beyond the executive directors to include firm-wide policy and particular oversight for the pay packages of the most highly paid non-board members.

The non-executive directors should convene regularly, as a body, with the chairman, but without their executive colleagues; and at least once a year they should meet on their own under the leadership of the senior independent director (see Section 10, below) to appraise the chairman's performance.

If the executive directors have a collective interest in any matter that goes to the board, the non-executives may effectively be left in control. This situation is commonly seen where a bid for the company is received from the management team, or from a private equity group with management involvement. The executives can play no part in the decision, and it will be for the independent directors to decide alone whether to recommend the bid to shareholders.

Walker also put a time commitment on the role in a major bank board: a minimum of 30 to 36 days a year for at least some of the non-

executives. The Code says that all directors must be able to allocate sufficient time to the company to perform their responsibilities effectively.
Less time will be needed for smaller companies and those with less
complex businesses, but, with a norm of 10 board meetings a year, additional committee meetings and off-site visits, the job should be no
sinecure.

8. Independent non-executive directors

The Code makes a distinction between non-executives who are independent and those who are not. To qualify for the former category, an
individual must not only have the necessary independence of character
and judgment but also be free of any connections that may lead to
conflicts of interest.

The Code makes it clear that someone will not normally be considered
independent if:

- they have been an employee of the group within the previous five
  years;

- they have a 'material business relationship' with the company or
  have had one within the previous three years, including an indirect
  relationship as a partner, director, senior employee or shareholder of
  an adviser or major customer or supplier (this would catch a partner
  from, for example, the company's audit firm moving on to the board
  after retirement);

- they receive remuneration from the company in addition to director's fees or they participate in the company's share option or
  performance-related pay schemes or they are members of the pension
  scheme;

- they have close family ties with any of the company's advisers, directors or senior employees;

- they hold cross-directorships or have significant links with other
  directors through involvement in other companies or bodies (this
  works against the 'old boys' club' method of appointing non-executives: George is finance director at company A and sits as a non-executive on the board of company B; Harry is chief executive at
  company B and sits as a non-executive at company A);

- they represent a significant shareholder;

- they have served on the board for more than nine years.

Ultimately, however, it is up to the board to decide who 'qualifies'. The board is expected to consider the above – and, indeed, any other factors that may impair independent judgment – but none of them is to be thought of as grounds for automatic 'exclusion'. It may be that an individual is judged to have the strength of character and integrity to remain unaffected by circumstances that, in theory, compromise their independence.

Sir David Walker, in his 2009 review of governance at major banks, argued for less emphasis to be placed on the independence of non-executive directors for the sake of it and for greater weight to be given to relevant financial industry experience. Independence in name was less important than 'the quality of independence of mind and spirit, of character and judgment'.

When they appoint non-executives, and each year when reporting to shareholders, the members of the board have to identify who is independent and who is not. If they have decided that, despite previous and/or current connections with the company, etc, an individual may be classed as independent, they need to explain the reasons why.

9. Composition and structure of the board

The Code states that:

> The board and its committees should consist of directors with the appropriate balance of skills, experience, independence and knowledge of the company to enable it to discharge its duties and responsibilities effectively – main principle B.1.

The provisions supporting this say that the board should have a 'strong presence' of both executive and non-executive directors so that no individual or small group can dominate its decision-taking. At least half the board, not counting the chairman, should be independent non-executive directors.

This means that a board of nine, for example, needs to have at least four independent non-executives to balance four executive directors, with the chairman being the ninth director.

An exception is made for a 'smaller company', defined as a company outside the FTSE 350 for the whole of the year before the year being reported on. Those smaller companies are urged to have at least two independent non-executive directors. (Indeed, they will need two if they are to comply with the Code's requirements for board committees – see section 15.)

Again, these principles and provisions are for guidance only: a company is free to explain why it believes such numbers of independent non-executives are excessive or not right for its own particular circumstances.

What does all this mean for the structure of the board? Does it effectively create two tiers? The Code is keen to stress that it still believes in the unitary board. The non-executives are not meant to comprise a separate supervisory body on, for example, the German model. Executive and non-executive, independent and chairman are all members of the single decision-making board at the heart of a UK company.

10. The senior independent director

The board should choose one of its independent non-executive directors to be the senior independent director. The 'SID' acts as an alternative point of contact for major shareholders who may have made little headway in discussions with the chairman, chief executive or finance director – or who may have concerns about the performance of such individuals. SIDs serve as a sounding board for the chairman and act as an intermediary for the other directors. The senior independent director also takes the lead in annual appraisals of the chairman.

The post caused some controversy when first proposed in 2003. It was argued that shareholders would be confused: should they talk to the chairman or the senior independent? And was there not a risk that, if they talked to both, different messages would be given – or a different spin given to the same facts? Also, chairmen saw the senior independents as muscling in on their patch. In practice, however, the role has kept a low profile and few problems have arisen. One exception occurred in the midst of the Marks & Spencer argument over Sir Stuart Rose's dual role as chairman and chief executive (see the box on page 70), when the SID let it be known that he was interested in taking on the chairman's job himself.

11. Appointment of directors

According to main principle B.2, there should be 'a formal, rigorous and transparent procedure' for the appointment of new directors. In other words, the days of putting your friends from the golf club on the board are long over.

The Code gives the recruitment task to a nomination committee, a majority of whose members should be independent non-executive directors.

There is no ban on the chief executive being a member – as is consistent with the committee's role in making recommendations for executive as well as non-executive appointments. The committee should be chaired by one of the independent non-executives or the company chairman, though he should stand aside when it comes to appointing his successor.

The committee is expected to:

■ evaluate the balance of skills, experience, independence and knowledge on the board and, in the light of that, draw up a description of the role it is seeking to fill and the capabilities required;

■ satisfy itself that there is succession planning in place for directors and senior management and to ensure 'progressive refreshing' of the board;

■ use external search consultancies or open advertising in the hunt for candidates for the chairman's role and non-executive posts (failure to cast the net this wide must be explained in the annual report);

■ make appointments only on merit and after assessing candidates by means of objective criteria;

■ ensure that candidates for the chairmanship and non-executive roles would have the necessary time to devote to the company;

■ set out the terms and conditions of the appointment of non-executive directors – including the expected time commitment and make those terms publicly available (usually on the company website).

Individuals who are non-executives in one company will often be executive directors in another – and vice versa. It's generally thought to be a good thing that an executive gets experience of the workings of another company and another industry. However, it's important that the demands on the individual are realistic – a major corporate dispute or a takeover can demand huge amounts of non-executive time. The Code says that the board should not agree to a full-time executive taking on more than one FTSE 100 company non-executive directorship or the chairmanship of such a company.

12. Induction and training for directors

Even experienced non-executive directors need training. This means an effective induction process when the director joins the board and an ongoing programme of professional development. In the words of main principle B.4, directors should 'regularly update and refresh their skills and knowledge'. They need both to understand the business they are running, its products, customers and suppliers, and to keep up with the pace of legislative and regulatory change.

'The company,' says the Code, 'should provide the necessary resources for developing and updating its directors' knowledge and capabilities.' Note also the obligation in Listing Principle 1: 'A listed company must take reasonable steps to enable its directors to understand their responsibilities and obligations as directors.'

The essential point is that directors must be given the right 'equipment' and get the right preparation to do their job. Their induction needs to be planned with care, with a programme over a number of months of site visits and meetings with both major shareholders and senior and middle management. The 2010 version of the Code gives the chairman responsibility for agreeing and reviewing a training plan for each director.

If the non-executives require outside advice to help with aspects of their job, the company should be prepared to pay for it. This can be especially relevant for the audit committee, where an independent view may be wanted on an abstruse accounting point. The Walker Report also emphasised the need for outside help when the non-executives are evaluating levels of risk in a complex business.

13. Evaluation

In the past few years, the idea of board-level appraisals has become increasingly accepted. Thus the Code's main principle B.6 says that 'the board should undertake a formal and rigorous annual evaluation of its own performance and that of its committees and individual directors'.

As with any appraisal process, the intention is that strengths are recognised and built upon and weaknesses are addressed – which may mean, ultimately, asking a director to go. Questions to ask will include:

■ Is the director's contribution to the board an effective one?

■ Do they demonstrate commitment to the role?

■ Are they giving the job the time it requires?

Once a year, the board should look at itself and assess what it does, its failures and successes; and a similar process should be conducted by the board for each of its committees.

The annual report needs to explain how these appraisals are carried out. In the past, many boards reported the use of home-grown procedures based on one-to-one interviews between the chairman and each director. In some companies, these fireside chats may have been less 'formal and rigorous' than intended, and from 2010 the Code has said appraisals should be externally facilitated at least every three years. Whatever is done, there needs to be transparency as to the process, with the annual report describing what has happened and any actions that resulted.

The chairman does not escape. His or her performance should be evaluated by the non-executives as a whole, under the leadership of the senior independent director. And they should consult the executive directors and take their views into account.

14. Re-election

A poor appraisal may result in the chairman asking a director to stand down. That will be an internal board matter. But what of the shareholders? What power do they have to get rid of directors who, in their eyes at least, have under-performed? Shareholders can pass a resolution at a general meeting to remove a director if they can muster more than half the votes cast. But in many companies, the AGM also gives the shareholders the opportunity to vote on the re-appointment of directors. Company articles will often provide that all new directors have to stand for re-election at the AGM following their appointment, and that is a provision echoed by the Code. Articles will also commonly stipulate that a third of the directors should retire and stand for re-election each year.

The Walker Report recommended that bank chairmen should stand for re-election every year. At the end of 2009, the FRC began a consultation offering two choices for all listed companies:

■ all directors (executive and non-executive) to be subject to re-appointment by the shareholders every three years (the position under previous versions of the Code), but the chairman to be subject to annual election; or

■ all directors to be proposed for re-election each year.

At the time of writing, the consultation had not closed, but several companies, BP included, had already decided on the latter option.

Examples of shareholders using their power to remove directors are few and far between. A memorable case occurred in 2004, with three Manchester United directors being shown the red card at the club's AGM. American sports tycoon Malcolm Glazer, who owned 28.1 per cent of the club's shares, took his revenge on those coming up for re-election after he was refused access to the company's books. (He later launched a successful bid for the whole company.)

The shareholders may not be privy to the detail of the board's appraisal of individual directors but the Code does require the chairman to confirm to them that, following an appraisal, the performance of the non-executive director up for re-election 'continues to be effective and to demonstrate commitment to the role'. Indeed, the board is required to tell shareholders why it believes an individual director should be re-elected.

The non-executive's letter of appointment needs to take account of the requirement that he or she stands for re-election at regular intervals. The Code says that two three-year terms should be the norm and a third, making nine years in all, should be 'subject to particularly rigorous review' and take account of the need for 'progressive refreshing of the board'. As we have seen in section 8, serving more than nine years raises the assumption of a lack of independence, which has to be rebutted each year by the board in the annual report.

Despite this, nine-year terms are common, and there is a widely held view that the rule should be dropped. Many companies would argue that there is little point in sacrificing a director's experience and knowledge of a group after only six years because of an unjustified fear that they may have gone stale. Once nine years are reached, the Code suggests that the director should be subject to annual re-election.

15. Board committees

The UK Corporate Governance Code requires a board to have three committees: remuneration, audit and nomination. Following the Walker review, banks and other financial institutions will usually also have a risk committee.

All of these committees should have terms of reference, and these should be publicly available (usually on the company's website).

In each case, the terms should set out clearly what the committee is to do, stating whether it is to take decisions or merely make recommendations. A remuneration committee will, in accordance with the Code's provisions, commonly have delegated authority to set executive pay. Its proposals will be discussed with the chairman and/or chief executive, and there may be a broad policy on directors' pay agreed with the board, but the responsibility will lie with the committee, not the board. By contrast, the nomination committee will usually make recommendations to the full board and leave the final decision to the board as a whole.

Membership of these committees is closely defined by the Code – see the next section for the rules on the audit committee, section 11 for the nomination committee and section 4 of Chapter 7 for the remuneration committee.

Nothing in the Code prevents executive directors, or indeed any other employee or outside adviser, being invited to attend a particular committee meeting. So the finance director may commonly sit in on audit committee meetings – the Code recognises that their presence will often be necessary and desirable. Likewise, the head of HR will often be needed at remuneration and nomination committee meetings. But neither has the right to attend or vote; they are only there by invitation.

The board may appoint further committees as necessary, either on a continuing basis to deal with ongoing matters (for example, treasury or compliance) or ad hoc to deal with a particular acquisition or matter of strategy. Many companies will have an executive committee made up of the chief executive and those who report directly to him or her but excluding the chairman and the non-executives. It may meet monthly or weekly and will have daily executive responsibility for the company's affairs.

16. Audit

The role of the audit committee is so important to good governance that it was subject to a separate review in 2003. The Smith Guidance on Audit Committees, produced by Sir Robert Smith, is annexed to the Code. Many of the provisions described below overlap with similar requirements in the FSA's Disclosure and Transparency Rules, which makes them mandatory, rather than just subject to the Code's more liberal comply or explain regime.

Composition of the committee

The Code provides that the audit committee should consist of at least three independent non-executive directors, or two for companies outside the FTSE 350. The chairman of a smaller company may be an additional member of the committee provided he was regarded as independent when he was appointed chairman, but he should not chair the committee.

The Code also says that the board should 'satisfy itself' that at least one member of the committee has recent and relevant financial experience. The Code is not specific about what constitutes 'relevant experience', but Smith says it means a professional qualification from one of the accountancy bodies. Failure to satisfy this requirement is one of the more common disclosures in company reports when detailing their compliance with the Code.

Often, the 'expert' will be a retired finance director from another company or a former partner of an accountancy firm. To comply with the Code's recommendations for independence, the board should, of course, exclude its own former finance directors and auditors. In any event, it must justify its choice in the annual report.

Given the complexity of the issues usually faced by an audit committee, it's essential that its members receive proper induction and training.

Roles of the committee

Main principle C.3 says:

> The board should establish formal and transparent arrangements for considering how they should apply the corporate reporting and risk management and internal control principles and for maintaining an appropriate relationship with the company's auditors.

The audit committee's main roles are elaborated in the Code principles, which can be summarised as:

■ to monitor the integrity of the company's financial statements and announcements;

■ to review internal financial controls and (unless there is a separate risk committee) risk management systems;

■ to monitor and review the internal audit function;

■ to recommend the appointment or replacement of external auditors and to review the effectiveness of their work;

■ to develop and implement policy on the use of the auditors for non-audit services.

They are discussed further below.

The audit committee is **guardian of the integrity of a company's financial statements** and performance. It must, in short, be satisfied that all figures presented to shareholders and the outside world will stand up to scrutiny and can be relied upon. This requires committee members not only to understand the financial statements and how they are made up (no mean feat as accounting standards get ever more complicated), but also to quiz the finance director and the external auditors as draft accounts are produced. Like all good non-executives, they must ask the right questions and be persistent if a satisfactory and intelligible answer is not forthcoming.

This general oversight of the company's accounts means that the audit committee also has a role in **checking the company's internal financial controls**, reviewing them and their operation and ensuring that necessary risk management systems are in place. Where a company has an **internal audit function**, the audit committee will need to extend its monitoring role to the internal auditors. Some of these roles may be performed by a risk committee, particularly following the recommendations in the Walker Report – the two committees will need to work closely together.

At least once a year, the committee should meet the internal and external auditors on its own (ie without management) so that any issues arising from their work can be freely raised. Between meetings, good communication must be maintained – particularly by the committee chairman. If there are no internal auditors, the committee should review each year whether there is a need for such a service; if it concludes there is not, it should explain why in the annual report.

The committee has some specific **duties in relation to external auditors**. It recommends the appointment of auditors to the board and approves their fees and the other terms on which they are retained. If there is dissatisfaction with their performance, it may recommend their replacement. In the very unlikely event that the board disagrees with the committee, the arguments on both sides need to be put forward to shareholders in the annual report and AGM papers. Smith also says that the committee should approve the appointment and removal of the head of internal audit.

The committee must keep a close check on the external auditors' independence and objectivity. Is it time for a change, if only to get fresh thinking and a new perspective on some old issues? Are the auditors getting too close to management?

Closely related to the second question is the issue of non-audit services. The independence of the auditors may reasonably be expected to be compromised if they also act as the company's consultants and advisers. Under the US Sarbanes–Oxley legislation (see the box on the following page), non-audit services such as consultancy and advisory work are severely limited. In the United Kingdom, it is left to the audit committee to decide what other services the auditors can provide. The committee needs to develop a specific policy on the matter – it may, for example, rule against some services as raising too many potential conflicts (for example, advice on remuneration policy), permit others (such as tax advice) and require a case-by-case decision on everything else. It may also require non-audit work above a certain financial limit to be approved by the committee.

Where non-audit services are performed, disclosures are required in the annual report, and the committee must explain how auditor objectivity and independence are to be preserved. The need to maintain independence and objectivity also means that the audit committee should develop a policy regulating the employment of former employees of the auditors.

The audit or risk committee also has a role in **fraud prevention**. It needs to be confident that there are opportunities throughout the company for employees to act as 'whistleblowers' and report improprieties and abuses. This may mean giving employees contact details for committee members for use if other avenues fail. Many companies have introduced confidential fraud hotlines for employees; others use an outside agency that can take calls and forward the information to the right person. A fraud response plan will be needed to guide investigations into any allegations of wrongdoing.

The Companies Act allows accountancy firms to limit their liability on company audits, but, as we have seen in the opening chapter, the limitation must first be agreed with the company and subsequently by the company's shareholders. Such agreements continue to be rare, but if they gain in popularity, negotiation of the limitation, and presentation of that agreement to shareholders for approval, is likely to be a new task for the audit committee.

The Sarbanes–Oxley Act

A detailed examination of the US Sarbanes–Oxley Act of 2002 (SOX), passed in the aftermath of the Enron and Tyco affairs and other corporate scandals, is outside the scope of this book. But no examination of corporate governance would be complete without reference to SOX and an acknowledgement that there are a few circumstances where it may affect UK companies and their directors.

SOX applies to all companies, whether incorporated in the United States or elsewhere, that publicly issue securities in the USnited States and file reports with the US Securities and Exchange Commission (SEC). That will include many large UK corporates with securities traded on the New York Stock Exchange. The Act has no direct application to other companies. However, US and non-US subsidiaries that fall outside its terms may be indirectly affected if their parents have to comply.

Among other things, the Act requires the chief executive officer and chief financial officer of a company to certify the annual and quarterly reports under separate civil and criminal provisions. Both must confirm that they have reviewed the reports and that there are no material mis-statements. Individuals who knowingly sign false certificates can face fines and severe criminal penalties. They can also end up forfeiting cash bonuses and share awards.

In addition, SEC rules require management to include a report on their internal controls and procedures for financial reporting in their annual reports filed with the SEC. Management must evaluate the effectiveness of those controls and procedures, and the company's auditors must issue a report on the assessment.

These requirements are likely to have a knock-on effect on directors and managers in UK subsidiary companies, who may be asked to provide similar certificates and confirmations in respect of their own financial reporting and internal controls. Such reports will give reassurance and perhaps some legal protection to US officers and management; at the very least, they will demonstrate that the US officers have asked the right questions and received replies that it is reasonable for them to rely on.

Because directors and managers of a UK subsidiary are not directly subject to the SOX provisions nothing they do or fail to do should constitute a breach of the Act or the SEC rules. Even if it did, the US authorities would have no jurisdiction to bring a prosecution in the United Kingdom (although the threat of extradition cannot be ignored).

Of course, giving a negligent, reckless or fraudulent certificate or report to the parent company may be regarded as an internal disciplinary offence and, in the worst cases, mean summary dismissal. A claim against the mis-reporting UK employee for any loss suffered in the United States cannot be discounted; reports and certificates requested from the United States should be prepared and verified with the highest standards of care.

The risks can be minimised if internal controls and procedures in a UK subsidiary mirror those in the US parent. Budgets and resources should be made available for such controls and procedures and, where necessary, for external advice and reports.

Resources and rewards for committee members

The audit committee needs to be adequately resourced. It should have access to outside advice when necessary. And the Smith guidance accepts that committee members should be paid further remuneration in addition to other fees to reflect the onerous nature of their duties and responsibilities. The chairman should command a higher level of remuneration than his colleagues.

Relations between the committee and management

The effectiveness of the committee is obviously closely linked to the effectiveness of senior managers. Management should not wait for the audit committee to ask for information. It needs to ensure that the audit committee is kept informed at all times and to take the initiative in supplying information to it.

17. Internal control

> The board is responsible for defining the company's risk appetite and tolerance. The board should maintain a sound system of risk management and internal control to safeguard shareholders' investment and the company's assets – main principle C.2.

The board needs to satisfy itself that it has appropriate systems to identify, evaluate and manage any significant risks the company might face.

The Code also recommends that the board (or the audit or risk committee) annually reviews the system of internal controls and reports to shareholders that it has done so (the FSA's Disclosure and Transparency Rules also require such a report). The review should cover 'all material controls, including financial, operational and compliance controls and risk management systems'.

The Turnbull Guidance (annexed to the Code) suggests ways of applying these principles. It acknowledges that risk-taking entrepreneurship is an essential part of any business and that the purpose of internal controls is to manage risk rather than to try to eliminate it. In other words, no system can guard against every adverse event, but a sound one can improve the chances of avoiding toxic assets or identifying a rogue trader, to quote just two recent examples.

The system of internal control needs to be an integral part of normal business processes. It needs to operate throughout the year: it should not just be a box-ticking exercise done every 12 months to keep the compliance officer happy. Since risks change as the company's business and the commercial environment in which it operates change, they must be reviewed and assessed regularly.

The Turnbull Guidance says that:

■ The board must set the company's policies for internal control; it is then up to management to implement those policies.

■ The policies must enable the company to respond to the risks it faces and so safeguard its assets against loss and fraud, and identify and manage the liabilities it faces.

■ The board (or an audit or risk committee) needs regularly to ask the right questions and to get the right answers to satisfy itself that the risks facing the company are being managed properly. This requires a good system of regular reporting throughout the company – so that important information from employees reaches the board.

The annual report needs to describe the system of internal control and explain any failure to comply with the Turnbull Guidance.

18. Relations with shareholders

Despite some impressions to the contrary, the Code makes it clear that good governance is not a one-way street. Companies and their boards have numerous obligations and duties to shareholders, but there are reciprocal duties owed by the shareholders to the company.

In the interests of good governance, investors should:

■ communicate with directors;

■ 'police' boardroom practices – ie monitor compliance with the Code.

Communication

Main principle E.1 says that there should be a dialogue between the board and shareholders 'based on the mutual understanding of objectives'. Yes, the board has to explain to shareholders what it is about, where it wants to get to and how it is going to meet its aims; but, equally, shareholders must make sure they clearly state their objectives and the timescale in which they want them achieved.

In talking about dialogue with shareholders, the Code refers largely to major investors. There are two reasons for this:

■ the Code originated as a response to pressure from large institutional shareholders for reform of boardroom practice;

■ practicalities dictate that no board is going to spend time or money talking to every shareholder with a few hundred shares: the priority will be investors with a large proportion of the share capital – and in most listed companies these will be pension funds, insurance companies and other investment managers.

While this focus on big investors is natural, perhaps even inevitable, it highlights a potential flaw in the Code. It could be seen as marginalising or ignoring those investors who, though small, still have rights. In many places, the Code openly refers to consultations with 'major shareholders'. An inconspicuous footnote maintains the legalities by stating: 'Nothing in these principles or provisions should be taken to override the general requirements of law to treat shareholders equally in access to information.'

The Business Review

All companies, public and private, need to produce a Business Review as part of their Directors' Report. The only exception is for 'small companies', which are defined as private companies that can satisfy any two of three conditions on turnover (not more than £5.6m), balance sheet total (not more than £2.8m) and employees (not more than 50). The purpose of the Review is to inform shareholders and help them to assess how the directors have performed their duty to promote the success of the company (see Chapter 2).

To that end, the Business Review must contain:

■ a fair review of the company's business;

■ a description of the principal risks and uncertainties facing the company;

■ a balanced and comprehensive analysis of the development and performance of the business during the year, and its position at the end of the year;

■ to the extent necessary to understand the business, an analysis using financial key performance indicators and other KPIs, particularly those on environmental and employee matters.

A UK listed company (not one whose shares are traded on AIM or PLUS) needs additional disclosures in its Business Review (to the extent they are necessary for an understanding of the business):

■ the main trends and factors likely to affect future development and performance;

■ information about the impact of the business on the environment, plus information on employees and 'social and community issues';

- information about people with whom the company has contractual or other arrangements that are 'essential' to the business.

That last point was a late amendment to the Companies Act 2006 and at the time came in for criticism from the business world. The government emphasised that it was designed to lead to disclosure of key relationships, such as reliance on a sole supplier or customer where the loss of a contract would have a serious knock-on effect. But contracts are not the only target: the government minister made it clear that key employees and even regulators may be essential to a business and could lead to disclosures.

One welcome relief is that no impending development or negotiation needs to be disclosed if that disclosure would be seriously prejudicial to the company. Nor is the Review subject to an audit, although directors will commit a criminal offence if they fail to comply with these requirements.

It's a difficult balancing act to maintain, keeping your major shareholders informed of the latest developments and consulting them on major issues of interest without putting them in a privileged position. Confidential briefings for analysts and major shareholders were criticised as being exclusive and unfair to small investors, and are now largely replaced by webcasts that any shareholder can log into, with copies of presentations by the chief executive available on a company's website.

The reality is that major shareholders will usually make their views known to the board by talking to the chief executive, the chairman or the senior independent director at what may be a regular meeting: the Code encourages non-executive directors to 'develop an understanding of the views of major shareholders' through face-to-face contact, briefings with brokers and analysts and surveys of shareholder opinion. Smaller shareholders have the forum of the annual general meeting where, if they are sufficiently vocal, their protests may hit the mass media and so apply pressure to the board in that way.

Compliance

In assessing a company's compliance with the corporate governance regime set out in the Code, Section E of its 2008 version urged institutional shareholders to 'give due weight to all relevant factors drawn to their attention'. They needed to factor into their assessment 'the size and complexity of the company and the nature of the risks and challenges it faces'. In other words, they had to adopt a proportionate response and understand the issues and considerations that would have influenced the board. Shareholders were not to adopt a box-ticking approach and ignore the explanations proffered by a board for non-compliance. Rather, they were to give the company their reasoned views if they disagreed and be prepared to enter into a dialogue with the board if differences remain.

Despite these strictures, the 2008–09 financial crisis laid bare continuing concerns on both sides that true engagement between companies and their shareholders was not always achieved. The Walker Report urged compliance with the Statement of Principles issued by the Institutional Shareholders' Committee in June 2007, upgraded to a code in November 2009 and available at the web address given at the end of this chapter. This sets out best practice for institutional shareholders in respect of their responsibilities to their investee companies. Subject to further discussions with interested parties, this code will replace Section E from June 2010.

In trying to police the board and exert pressure for reform, institutional shareholders need to ensure that they use the considerable voting power they have. There have been several cases where particularly vocal shareholders have failed to vote as a result, it would seem, of difficulties in passing instructions down the line to the nominees or agents who complete the proxy forms or attend the meetings on their behalf. One objective of the company law reform process, which resulted in the Companies Act 2006, was to 'enhance shareholder engagement', and to that end the government has taken (but not yet used) the power to compel institutional shareholders to disclose their voting records.

19. Corporate social responsibility

Although no part of the Code is specifically concerned with corporate social responsibility (CSR), there is some recognition that a company's duties extend beyond its shareholders:

> The board should set the company's values and standards and ensure that its obligations to its shareholders and others are understood and met – supporting principles, A.1.

Moreover, the Turnbull Guidance makes clear that risk assessment should cover not only narrow financial risks but also those related to 'health, safety and environmental, reputation, and business probity issues'.

The Companies Act 2006 adds to those pressures by requiring directors to have regard to community and environmental issues when considering their duty to promote the success of their company (see Chapter 2) and by the disclosures to be included in the Business Review (see box, page 86).

Increasingly, CSR is seen as part of best practice by both the City and the government. The Association of British Insurers, whose members own more than 15 per cent of the companies on the London Stock Exchange, publishes guidance on CSR-related issues for both companies and investors. Its 2007 'Socially Responsible Investment Guidelines' ask that the annual report highlights a company's environmental, social and governance (ESG) risks. A remuneration committee should also disclose whether it considers corporate performance on ESG issues when setting remuneration for senior executives, and whether an incentive structure may inadvertently encourage 'irresponsible' ESG behaviour.

The government sponsors a CSR website, on which it says it has 'an ambitious vision for UK businesses to consider the economic, social and environmental impacts of their activities, wherever they operate in the world'.

Most companies are keen to talk about social and environmental issues in their annual reports, and many argue that complying with CSR guidelines has become a commercial necessity. At the least, the growing number of 'green' and ethical investment funds needs to find 'green' and ethical businesses to invest in.

The charity Business in the Community claims a membership of more than 850 of the United Kingdom's top companies 'committed to improving their positive impact on society'. It publishes a Corporate Responsibility Index, which measures the performance of companies in terms of how well they apply CSR values to their business.

For bigger companies in particular, CSR is, it can be argued, not an add-on or an optional extra: it is an integral part of good governance.

Further Information; Useful Websites

The UK Corporate Governance Code
www.frc.org.uk/corporate

Governance materials in higher education
www.lfhe.ac.uk/governance/

The Good Governance Standard for Public Services
www.cipfa.org.uk/pt/download/governance_standard.pdf

The Myners review on the governance of mutual life companies
www.afs.org.uk/documents/MynersReview.pdf

The Institutional Shareholders' Committee – Code on the Responsibilities of Institutional Shareholders
www.institutionalshareholderscommittee.org.uk/library.html

The Institute of Directors publishes a book on best boardroom practice, *The Effective Director*. It also offers a wide range of information, advice and training for directors and boards.
www.iod.com

The Institute of Chartered Secretaries and Administrators publishes: guidance on matters reserved for the board; a sample non-executive appointment letter; guidance on the induction process for new directors; sample terms of reference for board committees.
www.icsa.org.uk/news/guidance.php

Information on corporate social responsibility appears on the Department for Business, Innovation and Skills website.
www.bis.gov.uk

The Quoted Companies Alliance represents the interests of smaller quoted companies (including those on AIM and PLUS).
www.quotedcompaniesalliance.co.uk

5

The FSA and Securities Regulation

The Financial Services Authority (FSA) was given four statutory objectives in 2000 when it was created by the Financial Services and Markets Act:

- to maintain public confidence in the financial markets;
- to promote public awareness of those markets;
- to protect the consumers of financial services;
- to reduce financial crime.

The 2008 banking crisis led the government to add financial stability as a fifth objective for the FSA.

The FSA has a variety of roles in pursuing these objectives: as the United Kingdom's financial services regulator; as the Listing Authority; and as the investigating and prosecuting authority for breaches of FSA rules, market abuse and other offences described in this chapter. Most firms and senior individuals working in the financial services sector or selling financial services products have to be FSA-authorised and are therefore FSA-regulated; all companies listed on the London Stock Exchange are subject to FSA rules; and anyone guilty of market abuse (explained in section 6 below) can face FSA censure and fines.

The reach of the FSA, therefore, is wide; its powers extensive.

Successful FSA enforcement action can mean:

■ Criminal liability – the authority pursues cases through the criminal justice system if it believes it 'appropriate' and in the public interest to do so. In 2008, continuing concerns about the prevalence of insider dealing led to a renewed emphasis on criminal prosecutions.

■ Heavy civil fines and/or public censure – the authority can levy unlimited penalties and issue public rebukes.

■ Denying individuals FSA-approved status and so preventing them from carrying out regulated functions.

■ Bad publicity and loss of reputation.

In 2008, the FSA described its enforcement strategy as one of 'credible deterrence', using enforcement action as one of its main tools to bring about real changes in behaviour to protect both consumers and markets.

The information given in this chapter – and the case studies that support it – should provide a guide to some of the circumstances that lead to FSA action against companies and their directors. Expert professional advice will, however, need to be sought in all cases.

1. Disclosure of price-sensitive information

For a stock market to work efficiently and fairly, two principles must apply: companies need to release relevant information as soon as it is available; and all those who want to deal in shares should have access to the same information at the same time.

Rules to that effect are contained in the FSA's Disclosure and Transparency Rules (DTR) and apply to companies with a full listing on the London Stock Exchange. The fourth of the FSA's Listing Principles ensures adherence to the spirit as well as the letter of the DTR: a listed company must communicate information to holders and potential holders of its listed equity securities in such a way as to avoid the creation or continuation of a false market.

The core obligation is set out in DTR 2.2.1: a company must notify the market, through an approved Regulatory Information Service (RIS), as soon as possible, of any inside information concerning the company. AIM companies are under a similar obligation, imposed by rule 11 of the AIM rules.

Inside information

For something to be classed as 'inside information', it must:

- be of a precise nature;

- not be generally available;

- relate (whether directly or indirectly) to investments traded on a UK regulated market (such as listed shares on the London Stock Exchange); and

- be likely to have a significant effect on the price of the shares if generally available.

The information needs to be specific to the company and there needs to be some certainty to it. Imprecise information, and news that is generally applicable, is not announceable; nor are conclusions or facts that can be gleaned from research or analysis, because any investor (in theory) has access to the same material.

Price sensitivity is crucial to the definition of inside information. A company must ask: would a hypothetical 'reasonable investor', out to maximise their own economic self-interest, be likely to use the information in making their investment decision? Information that will usually be considered relevant to a reasonable investor's decisions includes that affecting:

- the company's assets and liabilities;

- the performance of the company's business, or expectations as to that performance;

- the company's financial condition;

- the course of the company's business;

- major new developments in the company's business;

- information that has previously been disclosed to the market.

A commonly used rule of thumb is to say that a price movement of 10 per cent either way is 'significant' and so information that is unlikely to move the share price that much is not disclosable. But the FSA is very clear that there is no '10 per cent rule' and that price movements below that threshold can still be significant in particular cases.

Deciding whether information satisfies all these tests and should be announced to the market is often a difficult call for a board to make. The company's brokers or other financial advisers should always be consulted where there is doubt, particularly when considering the effect on the share price, as they will appreciate the factors likely to influence shareholders. Indeed, the FSA has criticised directors where the brokers' view has not been sought. Lawyers can help test the assumptions being made and take directors through the relevant definitions.

When an announcement is to be made, a company must take all reasonable care to ensure that any information it releases to the market is not misleading, false or deceptive, and that it does not omit anything that is 'likely to affect the import' of the information (DTR 1.3.4). If the decision is made not to announce, the matter should be kept under review and re-assessed as circumstances change.

The FSA monitors large share price movements, and an unexpected rise or fall will commonly result in a 'please explain' letter asking for the background circumstances. Professional advice should be taken before replying.

Delay

Inside information needs to be released to the market 'as soon as possible'; a delay of only a few days can be unacceptable (see the case notes on pages 96–99). Where the news is unexpected by the company, such as a natural disaster or a surprise contract loss, a short delay may be permissible to establish the facts. But if, pending the full announcement, there is a risk of a leak of confidential information, a holding announcement should be made, including as much information as is known.

Delay is permitted where public disclosure would prejudice a company's 'legitimate interests'. But there are conditions attached to this concession: the company must be sure that it can keep the information confidential and that leaks won't give some people an unfair advantage over others. Anyone who receives the information in the meantime must be under a duty of confidentiality to the company, whether as an employee, adviser or by specific agreement. And even where confidentiality can be maintained, the lack of an announcement must not be likely to mislead the public.

A company's legitimate interests will most commonly relate to its financial viability – if it is in negotiations with its banks and fighting for survival, it may be able to hold off announcing that it is having such discussions. But it will still need to disclose the fact that it is in financial difficulty – the exemption only applies to the negotiations, not to the underlying problem.

Market rumours

Where rumours are false or press speculation is groundless, a company is under no obligation to issue denials. Untruths can't amount to inside information.

But where rumours or speculation are largely correct, the company needs quickly to decide whether it has inside information that should be released. Once news has leaked, delay can no longer be justified, and directors need to ensure that the market is trading on the basis of accurate information that is available to all.

Lessons learned

In reaching the decisions on disclosure of price-sensitive information described in the case notes on pages 96–99, the FSA has drawn the conclusions below.

■ In respect of new developments in its sphere of activity, a listed company must first consider objectively the importance of those developments to the business and then, with its advisers (including its corporate brokers), objectively assess whether they may lead to a substantial movement in the company's share price.

■ In respect of a change in the performance of the business, a listed company must first consider objectively whether there has been such a change and then, with its advisers, objectively assess the likely price sensitivity of the change.

■ When looking at any change in its expectations of its performance, a listed company must first assess whether there has been a change in its subjective expectations (given the relevant facts) and then, with its advisers, objectively assess the likely price sensitivity of any change.

In addition, to minimise their exposure to, and the risk of, personal liability, directors need to:

■ make sure the company has a formal documented process to ensure compliance with its obligations under the DTR and the Listing Rules;

■ regularly review compliance with those rules and rigorously monitor changes to the company's financial condition, performance and its expectations of its performance;

■ ensure the company and the board are aware of the consensus of market expectations regarding the company's results and that they regularly ask whether the company's own expectations are in line with that consensus;

■ keep under review announcements already made and documents already published (such as audited accounts and previous trading statements) and consider whether any later developments may be material in the context of that information;

■ ensure that executive directors elevate issues to the full board without delay;

■ make sure that all members of the board, executive and non-executive, receive copies of the monthly management accounts and details of any major developments in the company's sphere of activity;

■ seek prompt advice from the company's corporate brokers, financial and other advisers as to whether any information or matter is price-sensitive.

Case Notes: Universal Salvage

Universal Salvage had a rolling contract with Direct Line Insurance for vehicle salvage that could be terminated on three months' notice. The contract was responsible for approximately 40 per cent of the vehicles handled by the company and for a significant proportion of its turnover.

Direct Line put the contract up for tender and, at a meeting on 18 March 2002, informed Martin Hynes, chief executive of Universal Salvage, that he had lost the business. The Universal Salvage board was told of this on 20 March 2002, and written confirmation of termination was received by the company on 25 March 2002. The termination was to take effect on 30 June 2002. Universal Salvage thought this was a negotiating ploy and wrote to Direct Line, stating the case for continuing the contract. Direct Line undertook to investigate the issues raised. Nevertheless, on 16 April 2002, Universal Salvage again received a letter that confirmed the loss.

In the meantime, Universal Salvage had been analysing the financial impact of the termination, for a presentation to the board on Thursday 18 April 2002. At that board meeting, it was decided that Hynes should seek advice from the company's financial adviser, WestLB, about the loss of the contract and the poor trading performance the company was experiencing in the final quarter.

The board meeting ended at 1.00 pm. Hynes telephoned WestLB at 4.30 pm and again at 5.00 pm but his usual contact was unavailable. Hynes got hold of him the next morning, Friday, and it was agreed that they would meet on Monday 22 April 2002. At that meeting, WestLB advised that an announcement should be made to the market about the lost contract and the poor trading figures. The announcement duly followed at 3.45 pm on Tuesday 23 April 2002; the company's share price fell by 55 per cent.

The delay of five working days in announcing the termination of the contract – from 16 April to 23 April 2002 – was determined by the FSA to be a breach of the obligation to disclose, as soon as possible, a major new development in the company's business. As from 16 April, the company needed to win significant amounts of new business to sustain previous levels of turnover and profit, and this, held the FSA, was a material fact, likely to lead to a substantial movement in the company's share price. The authority pointed to the 55 per cent drop in the share price to support its argument.

In addition, the FSA decided that Hynes was 'knowingly concerned' in the breach as he was the director best placed to take appropriate steps to ensure that the company notified the market without delay and he had failed to do so.

The company was fined £90,000; Hynes, £10,000.

Case Notes: Pace Micro Technology

On 8 January 2002, Pace announced its interim results but failed to reveal that its trade credit insurance for future deliveries to one of its largest customers had been withdrawn. The FSA judged this to be a breach of the obligation to ensure that information released to the market is not misleading and does not omit anything 'likely to affect the import' of information already released.

The regulator held that because two annual reports had previously stated that a credit insurance programme existed for large customers, the loss of cover was material and did affect 'the import' of the interim results announcement. It criticised Pace for not seeking sufficient advice on the matter. (The company had talked to its financial adviser but not its brokers.)

The FSA also found Pace to be in breach of the obligation to announce a change to the company's expectations for its revenue performance without delay.

The interim results showed that revenue for the year to 1 June 2002 would be broadly similar to the 2001 figure of £524m. On 4 February 2002, Pace revised its forecast to £455m but failed to inform the market of the change. The company argued that its earnings expectations had not changed (because the lost sales would have produced little or no profit) – and it is earnings, rather than revenue, that would usually be price-sensitive. It was not until 5 March that a trading statement was made – by which time things had deteriorated further and expectations had fallen to £350m. The news led to a share price fall of 67 per cent and wiped £462m from the company's market capitalisation.

The case underlines the need to include all material information when making announcements. The loss of the insurance cover was not deemed to be price-sensitive – just material to the matter being announced.

The FSA accepted that Pace had not acted recklessly or deliberately but had simply come to the wrong conclusion about what was material. The company was nonetheless fined a hefty £450,000 for breaching the two rules.

Case Notes: Wolfson Microelectronics

Wolfson Microelectronics supplies the semiconductors that are found in many digital consumer goods such as mobile phones and portable media players. Its largest customer generated 18 per cent of its 2007 revenue, but on 10 March 2008 Wolfson was told that it would not be supplying parts for future editions of two of the customer's products: $20m, or eight per cent of Wolfson's forecast revenue for the year, had disappeared.

But at the same meeting, Wolfson learned that there would be increased demand for parts going into a third product.

Two days later, Wolfson consulted its investor-relations advisers and the view was taken that no announcement was needed. Taking the good and bad news together, there would be no net change in revenues. There was also a concern that the market would overreact and, in any event, a non-disclosure agreement with the customer prohibited it from releasing the related positive news.

On 20 March, the Wolfson board met and, when one director took a contrary view, decided it needed legal advice. The lawyers agreed with the lone board member that the bad news was inside information and needed to be announced as soon as possible.

On the lawyers' advice, the brokers were also consulted on the likely impact on the share price. They confirmed that investors placed importance on the relationship with the major customer and that the shares were likely to suffer. Accordingly, the bad news was announced on 27 March; and the share price dropped 18 per cent.

The FSA held that, given the significance of the customer's business and the impact of the loss of supplies for the first two products, the bad news was inside information. A reasonable investor would have been likely to use it as part of his investment decision. There could be no offset of the negative against the positive news – each had to be looked at independently and announced where necessary. And if the bad news were likely to depress the share price, the company could not withhold the information because it thought the market would over-react or fail to understand the true value of the company.

The FSA was also clear that a confidentiality agreement was no excuse for not announcing price-sensitive information. (A well-drafted contract should in any event allow for announcements required by law or by a regulator; names can always be anonymised and the text agreed with the other party.)

The lawyers and the brokers should have been consulted earlier. The obligation to announce arose on 10 March and the 16-day delay was a breach of DTR 2.2.1. That meant there was a false market in Wolfson's shares in the intervening period, and so a breach also of Listing Principle 4.

Wolfson was fined £200,000, reduced to £140,000 for an early settlement.

Personal liability for directors

The FSA's main target in recent cases where there has been a failure to disclose inside information has been the company. But there is also a risk for directors if the FSA considers they were 'knowingly concerned' in the breach – the FSA can fine a director 'such amount as it considers appropriate'. The Universal Salvage case in 2002 (see page 96) suggested that the 'guilty' director did not need to have any intention to mislead the market: knowledge of the facts and some involvement in the breach were enough to result in a fine for the chief executive. In the later case of Pace, however, the directors escaped penalties and censure – the FSA seems to have accepted the idea that to 'be knowingly concerned' a director must have some awareness that the company is breaking the rules (see page 97).

The safest course will always be to make sure you know the rules and assume that absence of bad faith will not be enough to get you off the hook. In this context, Listing Principles 1 and 2 are very relevant:

■ a listed company must take reasonable steps to enable its directors to understand their responsibilities and obligations as directors;

■ a listed company must take reasonable steps to establish and maintain adequate procedures, systems and controls to enable it to comply with its obligations.

If the FSA cannot pin a breach of a specific listing rule or DTR on a company or its directors, it has the ability to pursue them for a breach of these listing principles. It can be all too easy, after the event, for the regulator to allege that the breach arose because directors did not understand their responsibilities and obligations, and that adequate systems were not in place for compliance. Ignorance of the law is no excuse.

Is it just the chief executive who is at risk of a fine? The short answer is 'no'. All directors of a listed company should accept full responsibility, collectively and individually, for the company's compliance with the rules. Although the FSA decided in the Universal Salvage case that the CEO had a particular responsibility, all directors, executive and non-executive, are under a duty to ensure the company complies with its obligations and to bring any price-sensitive information to the attention of the full board as soon as possible. And, as all these cases show, the FSA will take a dim view of the board that does not seek prompt advice from the company's brokers.

The rest of the board should not simply point to the CEO and expect him or her to take the rap in every case.

2. Disclosures in relation to shares

A director of a fully listed company is obliged to notify their company of any dealing in its shares within four business days, and the company must pass that information to the market by the end of the following business day. 'Dealing' is widely defined: the buying and selling of shares, the grant and exercise of options and pledging your shares as security for a loan are all disclosable. Similar rules apply to share dealings by directors of AIM companies.

In the case of a listed company, this obligation to disclose share dealings extends beyond directors to other 'PDMRs' – that is, persons discharging managerial responsibilities, namely senior executives who make management decisions and have regular access to inside information.

Prospectuses, listing particulars, admission documents and certain circulars produced by fully listed and AIM companies will also require details of directors' interests in the company's shares.

Where the company's shares are traded on the full list, AIM or PLUS markets, a director whose voting rights in the company's share capital reach three per cent or more has a separate obligation to give notice to the company of that interest. (This applies to all shareholders, not just directors.) The company must in turn make an announcement of the notifications it receives about such substantial interests in its shares.

3. Restrictions on dealings in shares

Directors of companies with shares quoted on a stock exchange are obliged not only to disclose details of their dealings, but also to observe restrictions on when they can buy and sell shares in their company. (There are few restrictions on when shares in an unquoted company can be bought or sold, but a director may have entered voluntarily into a 'lock-in' agreement not to sell their shares for a certain period, and many unquoted companies will have restrictions in their articles or in a share-holders' agreement that limit the ability to transfer shares freely.)

There are three separate regimes that potentially restrict a director or a senior manager of a fully listed company (or a director of an AIM company) from dealing in the company's shares:

■ the criminal offence of insider dealing;

■ the Model Code;

■ the civil market abuse rules.

These regimes can overlap: more than one of them might apply to a single set of facts. Moreover, their reach is potentially wide. They relate not just to directors but also to senior managers below board level, and indeed, in some circumstances, to any employee who has unpublished price-sensitive information about their company when they deal in its shares. A humble lab technician in a pharmaceuticals company who sees that the final tests on a new wonder drug are not going well might be just as liable as a director who deals before a profits announcement. So the rules on share dealing need to be widely known and understood throughout the organisation (for an example in another sector, see the Uberoi case on page 104).

4. Insider dealing

Insider dealing has been a criminal offence since 1985 and is currently set out in Part V of the Criminal Justice Act 1993. It continues, though, to be a tricky area. The FSA believes that professional insider dealing rings as well as rogue individuals exist within the City and are regularly trading on inside information not available to the rest of the market. The regulator has increased its enforcement work in recent years, but successful prosecutions are by no means straightforward.

The first legislation to create a level playing field for all investors proved ineffective. Since then, efforts have been made to tighten up the law and close the loopholes, but there remains a perception that some 'wrongdoers' continue to escape conviction.

The attempt to come up with effective legislation in this difficult area means the offence is a complex one to describe; what follows should be taken only as a summary of the main elements. References are made to shares, but the legislation also covers other company securities such as warrants, debentures, futures and contracts for differences.

A person will commit the criminal offence of insider dealing if they have inside information and:

■ that information is price-sensitive in relation to shares;

■ they deal in those shares, or encourage someone else to deal in those shares or pass inside information to another person;

■ the dealing takes place on a regulated market or through a professional intermediary such as a broker. (Included in the definition of a regulated market are exchanges elsewhere in the EU and some other overseas markets.)

'Inside information' has the same meaning described in section 1, namely information relating to a particular company that would, if published, be likely to have a significant effect on the price of shares in the company. It will not necessarily be about the company the insider works for: it might be about a supplier or a competitor – for example, news of the winning or loss of a big contract.

The insider will not commit the offence if they pass on general information about the market a company operates in, however confidential it might be. A director of a house building company might be liable if they give their dentist the unpublished information that group sales were significantly ahead of market expectations; but not if they disclose advance knowledge of a rise in mortgage rates.

There are several other defences available to someone charged with insider dealing:

■ they did not expect the dealing to result in a profit by virtue of the price-sensitive information;

- they reasonably believed that the information had been disclosed widely enough to avoid prejudicing other parties to the share transaction;

- the person who bought or sold the shares would have done so without the information – because they needed to sell the shares to raise the cash, or to come within a permitted dealing period, etc.

If successfully prosecuted, insider dealing can result in a fine and/or up to seven years' imprisonment.

Since 2008, the FSA has made greater use of its criminal powers, particularly in the case of insider dealing. In a speech delivered that year, its director of enforcement explained her belief that the threat of a custodial sentence was a much more significant deterrent than civil penalties in cleaning up UK markets. To that end, the FSA has recruited more senior lawyers experienced in criminal prosecution work and liaised more with other regulators at home and overseas.

In January 2008, the FSA brought its first criminal prosecution for insider dealing (see the box below), quickly followed by others. A major investigation into insider dealing rings was also begun, resulting in the execution of search warrants and the arrest of eight individuals.

Case Notes: Christopher McQuoid

Christopher McQuoid was a solicitor, employed as general counsel at TTP Communications. In May 2006, he was told confidentially that Motorola was planning a takeover bid for TTP. He passed that information to his father-in-law, James Melbourne, and two days before the deal was publicly announced, Melbourne bought shares at 13p each. The takeover price was 45p a share and Melbourne's profit was close to £50,000. Three months later, he gave a cheque for exactly half the gain to McQuoid.

Melbourne's trade was spotted as being suspicious and reported to the FSA. It prosecuted, and McQuoid was sentenced to eight months. Melbourne, aged 75, was given the same sentence, but suspended for 12 months.

Case Notes: Matthew and Neel Uberoi

Matthew Uberoi spent a six-month university placement at stock-broker Hoare Govett. While there, he learned confidential price-sensitive information about several of the firm's clients. He passed that information to his dentist father, who bought shares on the strength of it and made profits amounting to £110,000 as a result.

Both father and son were prosecuted for insider dealing. Matthew told Southwark Crown Court that his only knowledge of the offence came from films such as *Wall Street* and that the compliance training he received on joining the broker went over his head. 'When you are 20, you are just chuffed because there are biscuits on the table,' he told the FSA after his arrest.

The two were convicted, with Matthew receiving a 12-month prison sentence for passing the information on and Neel 24 months for using it.

Margaret Cole, the FSA director of enforcement, repeated her tough message: 'Insider dealing is not a victimless crime and we remain committed to stamping out this type of fraud.'

---

5. The Model Code

In order to reduce the risk that directors and senior managers of quoted companies might be thought to be taking advantage of inside information, both the Listing Rules and the rules of AIM require that companies restrict the times at which their directors and senior managers can deal in the company's shares. In the case of fully listed companies, the Listing Rules contain a 'Model Code' on share dealing by directors and senior employees that companies are required to adopt in full (though they may impose more onerous restrictions if they want).

Like the rules for disclosures in relation to shares (see section 2, page 100), the Code applies to both directors and other PDMRs and defines 'dealing' widely. If there is any doubt as to what is caught, seek advice.

Directors and other PDMRs must not deal in shares during a 'close period', that is the period of 60 days before the announcement of annual results or the publication of the annual report (or, if shorter, the period from the end of the financial year to the announcement or publication). In the case of half-year results, it is the time between the end of the half year and the date of publication. If a company reports quarterly, the close period is 30 days before each announcement or, if shorter, the period between the end of the quarter and publication. (The same restriction does not apply to the company's interim management statement, though a cautious approach would impose a similar 30-day ban on dealing.)

This is a simple prohibition: it is taken as read that, during those periods when financial results are being prepared, senior personnel are likely to have price-sensitive information.

Outside those periods, directors and other PDMRs are still prohibited from dealing if there is undisclosed inside information (see section 1, page 92). This might be news of a possible takeover, a significant share issue or a big contract win or loss.

Directors who want to deal in their company's shares must first get consent from their chairman or from another director appointed for the purpose. The same rule applies to the company secretary. If the chairman wants to deal, he should seek permission from the chief executive, and vice versa. Other PDMRs must apply to the company secretary or a director designated for the purpose. In each case, consent should not be given during a close period or when inside information exists, even if the person wanting to deal has no knowledge of it.

In any event, directors and other PDMRs should not deal in their company's shares on considerations of a short-term nature. An investment of less than one year's duration will be considered short-term, and consent to deal should always be refused in such a case.

These rules can be broken only where the person wanting to deal does not in fact have any inside information and can show they are in severe financial difficulty or there are other exceptional circumstances (such as a legal requirement to sell). In that case, the FSA has to be consulted before permission is given.

Requests for clearance and the consent or refusal should be in writing, and records should always be kept. Having been given clearance, you should deal as soon as possible and, in any event, within two business days. Miss that time limit, and you have to re-apply.

Directors and other PDMRs need to ensure that people connected with them, such as family members, and investment managers making investment decisions on their behalf, are aware of and follow these restrictions.

6. Market abuse

Background

The market abuse regime was introduced as a means of bringing more people who trade on inside information to justice. It sits alongside the criminal regime of insider dealing but operates with the lower standard of proof required for civil proceedings – the case has to be proved only 'on the balance of probabilities' rather than the higher criminal standard of 'beyond all reasonable doubt'. Because it is not a criminal offence, you cannot be imprisoned for market abuse, but you can face unlimited fines and/or public censure.

Market abuse is also much more loosely defined than insider dealing. So offences are more likely to be dealt with under the market abuse regime, though the FSA will bring a criminal prosecution where it has the necessary evidence.

Central to the meaning of market abuse is 'behaviour' in relation to shares and other financial instruments that are publicly traded, whether in the United Kingdom or elsewhere in Europe (see 'Scope' below). If that behaviour corresponds to one of seven types characterised as being either insider dealing or market manipulation, the civil offence may be committed and sanctions can follow. Note, however, that, in addition to these civil offences, both insider dealing and market manipulation remain criminal offences.

The regime will catch anyone who tries to 'abuse' the securities markets in the ways described, not just those working in the financial markets or who sit on the boards of quoted companies. Liability can arise even when the abuse was unintentional or committed indirectly – ie through the act of encouraging 'abusive' behaviour in another.

This section gives an outline of the market abuse regime. You should consult a financial services regulatory lawyer if you are in any doubt about whether a behaviour is caught by the rules.

Scope of the market abuse regime

The market abuse regime covers:

■ financial instruments (such as shares, warrants, futures, contracts for differences, options and debt instruments) traded on every regulated market in Europe (or for which an application for admission to trading has been made). In the United Kingdom, the relevant markets include the London Stock Exchange (both the full list and AIM), PLUS and commodity derivative markets;

■ all transactions relating to those instruments, even if they are carried out off-market.

In certain circumstances, behaviour in respect of other, related, instruments or underlying commodities is also caught, even if those instruments are not themselves traded on a regulated market. Behaviour involving securities traded on a foreign unregulated market may be caught if an option linked to them is traded in London.

The seven behaviours

There are seven types of behaviour defined as forms of market abuse.

■ **Insider dealing** – dealing or an attempt to deal, by an insider, in an investment on the basis of inside information.

■ **Improper disclosure of inside information** – disclosure by an insider of inside information to another person otherwise than in the course of their employment, profession or duties.

■ **Misuse of information** – behaviour that is both:

(a) based on information not generally available to those using the market but likely to be seen by 'regular users' as relevant when deciding the terms on which transactions in investments should be made; and

(b) likely to be seen by regular users as below reasonable or acceptable standards.

■ **Manipulating transactions** – participating in transactions or orders to trade that give, or are likely to give, a false or misleading impression as to the supply, demand, price or value of a qualifying investment or related investment, or that secure the price of such an investment at an abnormal or artificial level.

■ **Manipulating devices** – participating in transactions or orders to trade that employ fictitious devices or any other form of deception or contrivance.

■ **Disseminating information likely to give a false or misleading impression** – the act of spreading, or causing the spread of, information about a qualifying or related investment by a person who knew or could reasonably be expected to have known that the information was false or misleading.

■ **Market distortion** – behaviour that is likely to be seen by a regular user of the market as a failure to observe the standard that could be reasonably expected in the circumstances and that either:

(a) gives, or is likely to give, a regular user of the market a false or misleading impression as to the supply, demand, price or value of a qualifying or related investment; or

(b) could be regarded by a regular user as distorting, or being likely to distort, the market in that investment.

There are some 'safe harbours' from market abuse. Some actions will not be caught if they comply with other rules – for example, certain provisions of the Takeover Code and the Listing Rules. The FSA's Code of Market Conduct, which can be accessed via the FSA website, sets out further guidance on what is and what is not market abuse.

Case Notes: Examples of Market Abuse

The following are real-life examples of the FSA taking action against market abuse, showing the risks that companies and individuals can face. They cannot be taken as definitive statements of the law in the same way as a case decided by a court. But they do show the view taken by the FSA of certain conduct and illustrate the penalties that can be imposed.

A simple, and blatant, example of misuse of information market abuse is seen in the case of James Parker. He was the financial controller at **Pace Micro Technology**, and the facts of the case revolve around the problems described on page 97. With the benefit of inside information and in clear breach of the company's share dealing rules, Parker not only sold shares ahead of a profit warning that led to a dramatic fall in the company's share price, but also carried out an active programme of spread bets on the share price, making an aggregate profit of £121,742. His claim that this was part of an existing trading strategy uninfluenced by his inside information was not believed, and in August 2006 he was fined £250,000.

A civil case of **insider dealing** was brought against two traders at **Dresdner Kleinwort**. They managed a portfolio that held $65m of a Barclays floating rate note (FRN) issue. In March 2007, they were given inside information about a possible new issue of Barclays FRNs on more favourable terms and immediately off-loaded their existing holding to other investors who were unaware of the Barclays proposal. That afternoon, the new issue was announced, and the purchasers made losses of $66,000. The traders argued that, in the debt markets they dealt in, what they had done was acceptable practice. They escaped with a censure and no fine – in recognition, perhaps, that there was some basis for their claim.

The £17m fine levied against **Shell** in August 2004 for market abuse and breach of the Listing Rules set a new FSA record. In early 2004, Shell announced that it was writing down 25 per cent of its hydrocarbon reserves, causing a £2.9bn drop in its market capitalisation. The FSA found that the company had not only **disseminated information likely to give a false or misleading**

impression in relation to its reserves since 1998 but also failed to act when evidence of irregularities first came to light. Executives had been aware of the problems at least four years previously. Nonetheless, the FSA's fine appeared puny compared with the $120m (£66m) settlement agreed with the SEC, its US equivalent. Having ruled against Shell, the FSA continued its enquiries into the conduct of a number of individuals in the senior management at the company, most notably the former chairman, Sir Philip Watts. But in November 2005 it announced that no further action would be taken. The company may have been at fault, but no one individual was found to have committed market abuse.

Market distortion led to a fine of £500,000 for **Evolution Deeson Gregory (EBG)**, the financial services group, and of £75,000 for its head of market making. EBG also paid £150,000 in compensation to investors. In autumn 2003, the company had short sold more than twice the entire issued share capital of an AIM listed company with, in the FSA's view, no reasonable plan for ensuring it would be able to deliver the shares it had sold. An expected issue of new shares did not materialise; 250 investors failed to get the shares they thought they had bought. EBG's trading led to a serious distortion of the market, resulting in the suspension of the shares on AIM.

Critical factors in determining penalties

When deciding the type of penalty for market abuse, the FSA says it will look at a number of factors. These include:

■ the nature and seriousness of the suspected behaviour;

■ the conduct of the person concerned after the behaviour was identified;

■ the degree of sophistication of the users of the market in question, the size and liquidity of the market, and the susceptibility of the market to abuse;

■ whether sufficient action has been taken by other regulatory authorities;

■ action taken by the FSA in previous similar cases;

■ the impact, given the nature of the behaviour, that any financial penalty or public statement may have on the financial markets or on the interests of consumers;

- the likelihood that the same type of behaviour (whether on the part of the person concerned or others) will happen again if no action is taken;

- the disciplinary record and general compliance history of the person who has committed the market abuse.

The FSA can impose unlimited fines on companies and individuals found to have committed market abuse. Other sanctions include: a public statement that a person has engaged in market abuse (as in the Dresdner case, page 108); a court injunction to prevent any repeat; a requirement to give up any profits made or to pay compensation to the victims of any abuse (as in the EBG case, page 109). (The victims have no right of direct action against the abuser under the market abuse legislation.)

7. Market manipulation

Both insider dealing and market manipulation are types of market abuse under the civil regime described above; but each is also a criminal offence (see section 4 for insider dealing).

A person will be guilty of market manipulation if they commit any act or engage in any conduct that creates a false or misleading impression as to the market in any investments, or their price or value, and they do it with the intention of:

- creating such a false and misleading impression; and

- inducing another person to deal (or not deal) in those investments.

The 'classic case' is that of the share ramping operation, whereby a party drives up a company's share price by buying heavily and so creating a false impression of the demand for the shares – perhaps to influence a takeover where the shares are being used to settle part of the offer price.

Market manipulation, when prosecuted as a criminal offence, can mean an unlimited fine, a prison sentence of up to seven years, or both.

It should be emphasised, though, that there has to be a clear intention on the part of the accused to mislead and for others to rely on the misleading impression. It is a defence to show that you reasonably believed that you would not create a false impression; evidence of full public disclosure of what was being done and by whom will greatly assist your case.

Other defences apply where the action was taken in accordance with rules to control the issue of information (such as the Listing Rules) or in connection with a buyback of shares.

8. Misleading statements

A further criminal offence seeks to catch those who make misleading statements in the financial services sector.

A person can be liable if they:

■ make a statement, promise or forecast that they know to be materially misleading, false or deceptive;

■ recklessly make such a materially misleading, false or deceptive statement, promise or forecast – whether they are dishonest or not;

■ dishonestly conceal any material facts in a statement, promise or forecast.

In each of these cases, the person will be guilty if either of the following applies:

■ they made the statement for the purpose of inducing another to buy or sell shares or enter into any other type of investment agreement or to exercise (or refrain from exercising) any share rights;

■ they were reckless as to whether the statement would have that effect.

Some of the most obvious cases occur when a company is floating on the stock market. Directors will commit the offence if a statement or a forecast in a prospectus that they know to be false induces investors to take up the shares; or if they are reckless as to whether the statement or forecast is false – that is, they have taken no care in establishing the truth and have simply shut their eyes to the misleading nature of what is said. Boards and their advisers must take extreme care in producing these types of document, verifying each and every statement that could influence the behaviour of investors. The same applies to documents sent to shareholders on a company takeover, whether by the bidder or the target.

Like market manipulation, the offence is punishable by up to seven years in prison and/or an unlimited fine. But directors who make misleading statements face more than criminal liability. They may also be liable for compensation to investors who lost money (see the following case notes box).

Case Notes: AIT

Both imprisonment and a compensation order were the consequences for two directors of AIM company AIT in the first case brought by the FSA under the law on misleading statements. Carl Rigby and Gareth Bailey issued an announcement stating that the company's turnover and profit were in line with expectations. Those expectations depended on revenue from three specific contracts. The problem was that the contracts did not exist.

In August 2005, Rigby and Bailey were convicted at Southwark Crown Court of recklessly making a statement that was misleading, false or deceptive and were sentenced to three-and-a-half and two years respectively (reduced to 18 and nine months on appeal).

The Court of Appeal upheld a compensation order against Rigby of £208,796 and a costs order of £250,000; Bailey had to pay the more modest sum of £35,114.

---

9. FSA enforcement procedures

Powers

When investigating cases like the ones detailed above, the FSA has a number of statutory powers to assist it.

It can obtain information that is relevant to the investigation; it can, in some circumstances, detain people for questioning and call on the police to arrest suspects. Those who are seen to impede or obstruct its investigations can face stiff penalties.

The FSA says that it will make it clear in each case whether it is using its statutory powers or not. Where it is not, there is no obligation to produce documents or to attend an interview or to give answers when questioned.

Use of the statutory powers is, however, standard practice. In most cases, parties will be compelled to produce documents and answer questions in interview – even if they are willing to cooperate voluntarily.

Consistent use of its statutory powers is, the FSA believes, fairer and more transparent and efficient for all concerned.

So finding oneself on the wrong end of the FSA's use of its powers of compulsion does not mean that you are suspected of anything or viewed as being hostile; even innocent witnesses are likely to be subject to this standard practice.

But the FSA is equally clear that ready cooperation in attending an interview and answering questions may well result in a more lenient penalty should misconduct be found. Where the statutory powers are used, a failure to attend an interview, as Christopher Westcott found (see the following box), will be a contempt of court punishable by a fine, imprisonment or both, as will a failure to answer questions or to produce documents. There is, in effect, no right to silence. And there is no equivalent to the US citizen's right 'to plead the fifth' – that is, to protect yourself against self-incrimination.

The FSA's powers are undoubtedly extensive, but it says it takes a risk-based approach and will only pursue those cases that are in line with its overall priorities and where it is important to send out a message to the market or where breaches are particularly serious.

Case Notes: Christopher Westcott

In October 2003, Christopher Westcott, owner of Durham-based company Cathedral Funeral Services, was given a 28-day suspended prison sentence by the High Court for failing to cooperate with an FSA investigation. The authority had been investigating Westcott, suspected of selling funeral plans without proper authorisation and using a number of aliases to do so, since April 2002. His sentence was suspended only on the condition that he subsequently complied with the FSA's requirements.

In 2006, Westcott was jailed for three-and-a-half years for theft related to the same funeral policy scam.

Settlement

A party under investigation can, at any point, open settlement discussions with the FSA and so spare itself the time, expense and bad publicity of further investigation. The FSA gives credit in deciding penalties for early cooperation and acceptance of fault. So Wolfson Microelectronics (see case notes, page 98) had its fine discounted by 30 per cent because it agreed to an early settlement. In the Shell case (see market abuse box, page 108), the fine of £17m would have been 'significantly higher', the FSA said, had it not been for the company's high degree of cooperation. (Interestingly, though, Shell did not admit it was at fault.)

Decisions and appeal

If, having made investigations, the FSA decides to pursue a matter, it will take it in the first instance to its Regulatory Decisions Committee (RDC). Staffed by current and recently retired City practitioners as well as by lay members, the RDC oversees the enforcement process; it examines cases and takes representations from parties under investigation. If the firm or individual concerned accepts the committee's decision, it takes effect. If there is no acceptance, and the FSA issues a decision notice, the accused can refer the matter to the Financial Services and Markets Tribunal, an independent body run by the Tribunals Service, part of the Ministry of Justice. Tribunal hearings are conducted from scratch. They usually, however, take place in public – a fact that may argue in favour of settling the case with the FSA.

6

Service Contracts

This chapter focuses on the major issues for employing companies and individual directors when agreeing service contracts and when negotiating termination packages. More details on the design of remuneration packages and on pension provision follow in Chapters 7 and 8.

1. The general legal and regulatory framework

Directors and employers clearly do not start with a clean sheet of paper when negotiating a contract. There are several legislative, regulatory and other provisions that determine what is lawful and/or prudent, particularly in the case of a listed company. The following factors should be borne in mind.

- Directors have, as Chapter 2 makes clear, a duty to promote the success of the company at all times. When negotiating and agreeing service contracts, they need to ensure that their conduct is consistent with this duty.

- The Companies Act imposes certain constraints on the length of notice periods and fixed terms.

- The Companies Act also requires listed companies to make full disclosure of directors' rewards in a remuneration report on which shareholders have an advisory vote at the AGM. (Large votes against the report always mean bad publicity – see the box on investor activism in the following chapter, page 142.)

■ The UK Corporate Governance Code, which applies to all listed companies, imposes requirements regarding the source of instructions (see section 2, below), the length of notice periods and fixed terms, the make-up of the remuneration package and the negotiation of termination packages.

■ The Institutional Investors' Corporate Governance Statements set out details of the approach institutional investors expect companies to take in relation to the length of notice periods and fixed terms, the make-up of the remuneration package and severance packages.

■ The 'Joint Statement' by the Association of British Insurers (ABI) and the National Association of Pension Funds (NAPF), issued on 18 February 2008, sets out guidelines on executive contracts and severance.

So listed companies are increasingly expected to comply with requirements over and above those laid down by statute – ie with the recommendations of the Corporate Governance Code – and to respect the views of institutional investors, whose stewardship role was emphasised by the 2009 Walker Report (see Chapters 4 and 7). Thus, notice periods shorter than 12 months are becoming common. (As Chapter 4 makes clear, the Listing Rules require companies either to comply with the detailed provisions of the Code or explain, in the annual report, why they have not done so.)

The service contract between an employer and a director is both a legal agreement and an incentive tool: it's also the focus of many corporate governance concerns, particularly on 'rewards for failure'. The Joint Statement by the ABI and the NAPF concludes: 'It is unacceptable that poor performance by senior executives, which detracts from the value of an enterprise and threatens the livelihood of employees, can result in excessive payments to departing directors. Boards have a responsibility to ensure that this does not occur.'

2. General principles of negotiation; source of instructions

There are two key legal and regulatory points.

A director should not be personally involved in their own service agreement and remuneration package.

This means that they should not be responsible for preparing or instructing the company's lawyers in relation to their own contract and should not be involved in the company's decision making about their own service agreement/remuneration.

There should be clarity about who has responsibility for negotiating service agreements and remuneration packages for directors.

As part of a 'formal and transparent procedure' for the development of executive remuneration policy and for the setting of the pay packages of individual directors, the Corporate Governance Code requires that (on a comply or explain basis):

■ The board establishes a remuneration committee of at least three, or, in the case of a smaller company, defined as a company outside the FTSE 350, two members. (The company chairman may be a member if previously classed as 'independent'; the other members should all be independent non-executive directors).

■ Remuneration committees have delegated responsibility for setting remuneration for all executive directors and the chairman, and this extends to pension rights and any compensation payments (see Chapter 7, section 4).

3. Length of fixed terms and notice periods

Specifics of law and regulation

The Companies Act 2006 says that:

■ Contracts of more than two years' duration need to be approved by shareholders in general meeting. In the absence of such an approval, the term is void and the contract terminable on reasonable notice.

■ A director's contract (whatever its duration or notice period) must be available for inspection by shareholders.

Under the code of directors' duties, contained in the 2006 Act:

■ Where a contract provides for a particularly long term there is the risk of a challenge by shareholders on the grounds that, in agreeing to the provision, the directors failed to put the company's interests first and consequently were in breach of the code of directors' duties. (It is therefore advisable for any board/remuneration committee employing directors on long-term contracts to minute the reasons why.)

Under the Listing Rules:

■ A listed company's report to shareholders on directors' remuneration must include details of any service contracts with a notice period of more than one year or with provisions for pre-determined compensation on termination that exceed one year's salary and benefits, giving the reasons for such a notice period/pre-determined compensation.

The UK Corporate Governance Code says that:

■ notice or contract periods should be set at one year or less;

■ if it is necessary to offer longer notice or contract periods to new directors recruited from outside, such periods should reduce to one year or less after the initial period.

Negotiation points

From the employing company's perspective

Notice periods and fixed terms that exceed 12, perhaps even six, months may not be in the company's best interests – irrespective of the seniority and importance of the director. There are several reasons why:

■ **They are impractical:** few companies want directors who have decided to leave continuing to work for them for a long period. They will usually agree to allow the director to go before their notice expires – or put them on 'garden leave' (but enforcing garden leave for more than six months can be difficult; see section 6, page 127).

■ **They have cost implications:** the longer the notice period, the larger the potential pay-off if the company chooses to terminate the employment.

■ **They can antagonise investors:** institutional and other shareholders prefer shorter notice periods and fixed terms so as to limit the company's exposure on termination.

The argument that lengthier periods are necessary to attract high-calibre people seldom holds water. Top-performing individuals do not need the security of long contracts: they can reasonably be expected to find another position within six months and so mitigate their losses. If there are exceptional circumstances that justify a longer term, it may, as the Corporate Governance Code advises, be best to reflect this through an initial term followed by a shorter notice period.

Long notice periods and fixed terms look anachronistic. A 2005 Deloitte report for the government on the impact of the Directors' Remuneration Report Regulations concluded that there had been 'a rapid and almost complete reduction in directors' notice periods to one year or less'. The report included data showing that while 32 per cent of FTSE

100 directors had notice periods of two years in 2001, this had fallen to just one per cent by 2004.

In the Joint Statement, the ABI and NAPF say: 'We believe that a one-year notice period should not be seen as a floor, and we would strongly encourage boards to consider contracts with shorter notice periods. Compensation for risks run by senior executives is already implicit in the absolute level of remuneration, which mitigates the need for substantial contractual protection.'

From the director's perspective

For a director, a lengthy notice period can be a double-edged sword. On the one hand, it provides financial security should things go wrong. On the other, it acts as a straitjacket: combined with a well drafted garden leave provision, the notice period gives the company a hold on the director and can be used to limit their ability to move to an attractive position with another company.

Much will depend on personal circumstances. Where a director has concerns about their ability to secure another position quickly, perhaps because of their age or the economic climate, then it is in their interests to negotiate as lengthy a notice period as possible. Where a director is very confident about their position in the marketplace, and possibly sees their current job as a stepping stone to greater things elsewhere, a shorter notice period may be desirable.

In negotiations, the following are likely to be relevant.

■ **Current notice:** someone who has previously enjoyed the security of a six months' notice period may reasonably expect the same from a new employer.

■ **Risk:** if the director is being recruited into a new sector, they may argue for a longer notice period on the grounds that it will be more difficult for them to secure another position swiftly. They may also want added security if the company has a reputation for hiring and firing directors, is in a particularly volatile marketplace or is otherwise unstable.

■ **Reward:** sometimes the director is lured by the promise of 'jam tomorrow'. Where, for example, the company has plans to float on the Stock Exchange, the director will want to know they will be employed long enough to reap financial benefits.

From both perspectives

It is important that both the company and the individual director understand exactly what has been agreed in relation to the contract term. They should, therefore:

- avoid jargon when negotiating/instructing lawyers – the meaning of terms such as 'rolling' or 'evergreen' contracts is often disputed between employment lawyers;

- be very precise about how the notice period/fixed term should work;

- make any provision as simple to understand and operate as possible;

- avoid complex arrangements whereby notice can only be served on particular dates/during particular periods, etc.

4. Payment in lieu clauses

Purpose

A payment in lieu clause allows an employer to terminate someone's employment instantly on making a payment in lieu of salary or salary and benefits during a notice period or, possibly, a portion of the salary otherwise due.

It means more flexibility for the employer, entitling a company to bring an employment relationship to an end and quickly introduce a replacement.

Without it, companies that dismiss with no notice are in breach of contract and therefore at risk of legal action – ie a claim for wrongful dismissal.

Payment in lieu provisions are particularly important where:

- the contract has restrictive covenants (see section 6, page 127) – these cannot be relied upon in cases of wrongful dismissal;

- the director holds equity in the company and the amount they are entitled to be paid for a return of their shares depends on whether they have been wrongfully dismissed/how long they have been employed before termination.

Tax implications

Where a payment is made by a company under a payment in lieu provision it is regarded by HM Revenue & Customs as an emolument deriving from the employee's employment contract. This means that the £30,000 tax exemption for a severance payment will not be available: the full amount of the severance payment (or at least that portion representing the payment in lieu) will be liable for tax and National Insurance.

Negotiation points

Payment in lieu provisions need very careful drafting and will frequently be the subject of negotiation. Advice should be sought from an employment lawyer, but companies should bear in mind the points below.

■ It should be absolutely clear that payment in lieu will be at the discretion or election of the company. Otherwise, a director will be able to argue that they are automatically entitled to a payment in lieu where the company chooses to terminate. The courts have made clear that where an entitlement under a payment in lieu provision has arisen, an employee can receive the appropriate sum as a debt without deduction for mitigation or accelerated receipt. This means it is in the company's best interests for payment in lieu to be optional; in some circumstances, it may be preferable to dismiss instantly and then negotiate a package, taking proper account of mitigation.

■ Care should be taken when deciding the amount of the payment or the formula to calculate it. The company may wish to negotiate (or be seen to negotiate) a payment in lieu provision that does take some account of mitigation – ie an executive's likely losses on termination. This is often achieved by including a formula where a payment in lieu only reflects salary, not salary and benefits. But if a director is to be employed on a lengthy notice period, a company may want to include further provision for mitigation. Another option is to draft the provision so that the company can elect to make the payment in lieu in instalments, the right to such payment terminating on the director starting in a new position.

■ The instalment option is supported by the Joint Statement: 'Phased payments are generally appropriate for fulfilling compensation on early termination. The ABI and NAPF are not supportive of the liquidated damages approach, which involves agreement at the outset on the amount that will be paid in the event of severance.'

5. The remuneration package

Legal and regulatory background

Directors' service contracts must be drawn up with regard to both legal and regulatory provisions on pay. This means being aware not only of restrictions on directors' involvement in decisions about their own contracts (see section 2, page 116), but also of best practice guidelines for listed companies on pay levels and the make-up of the pay package. The UK Corporate Governance Code calls for a balanced package that pays no more than is necessary to attract, retain and motivate the top talent and avoids an 'upward ratcheting' in executive pay. 'Balanced' means having the right mix of fixed and variable (often performance-related) elements. (See the following chapter, section 6, page 152.)

Basic salary

The company should bear several points in mind.

■ Articles of association will often limit the amount the company can pay in directors' fees. The service contract should therefore make clear that salary payable is inclusive of any fees or other remuneration to which the director may be entitled from the company or any group company. This will avoid argument over how much remuneration is referable to fees and enable the company to comply with any limits.

■ Provisions regarding salary reviews – when they will take place, how they will be carried out – should be set out clearly to avoid future dispute. If a contractual right to an increase is not intended, there should be wording making this clear.

■ The practice of increasing directors' pay shortly before retirement and thereby significantly increasing their entitlement under a company's final salary scheme carries risks. It could be deemed to be against the company's best interests. The Corporate Governance Code provides that: 'The remuneration committee should consider the pension consequences and associated costs to the company of basic salary increases and other changes in pensionable remuneration, especially for directors close to retirement.'

Bonus

To avoid future dispute, both the employing company and an individual director need to ensure that bonus provisions are clear and fully understood. The key points to remember are listed below.

■ The first major issue to determine is whether the director will have a clear-cut contractual entitlement to a bonus according to a particular formula or merely a right to be considered for a bonus by the board/remuneration committee. If the intent is the latter, very careful drafting will be needed.

■ An employing company also needs to be aware that, even where a bonus scheme is discretionary, there will be constraints on the decisions that can be made. This follows the High Court case Clark v Nomura in which it was held that 'even a simple discretion whether to award a bonus must not be exercised capriciously' and an employer should not exercise its discretion in an 'irrational or perverse way' – ie a way in which 'no reasonable employer would have exercised its discretion'.

But this does not make it easy for an employee to challenge bonus decisions (see case notes in the following box).

Case Notes: Commerzbank AG v Keene

The 2006 case of Commerzbank AG v Keene, in which a very high paid investment banker sought to challenge the level of his bonus, shows that the courts are generally reluctant to review an employer's decision on the level of a discretionary award.

The Court of Appeal said that:

> It would require an overwhelming case to persuade the court to find that the level of a discretionary bonus payment was irrational or perverse in an area where so much must depend on the discretionary judgment of the bank in fluctuating market and labour conditions.

While this decision concerns discretionary bonuses in the investment banking sector, it is significant in relation to discretionary bonuses generally. Most companies, after all, operate in fluctuating market and labour conditions.

■ Decisions regarding the level of discretionary bonus payments are prone to allegations of discrimination. A particularly high profile instance of this was the case of Bower v Schroder Securities Limited, in which a senior investment banker was awarded £1.4m in compensation for what (in her words) was an 'insultingly low' award. (She received a bonus of £25,000 when comparable male colleagues were awarded £440,000 and £650,000.)

■ Board/remuneration committees should also take into account Corporate Governance Code guidance in Schedule A, which underlines the link between pay and performance:

The remuneration committee should consider whether the directors should be eligible for annual bonuses. If so, performance conditions should be relevant, stretching and designed to enhance shareholder value and to promote the long-term success of the company. Upper limits should be set and disclosed. There may be a case for part payment in shares to be held for a significant period.

■ Additionally, board/remuneration committees should consider the Joint Statement, which says that:

From the outset, boards should establish a clear policy to ensure any non-contractual payments are linked to performance. No director should be entitled to discretionary payments in the event of termination of their contract arising from poor corporate performance. Remuneration committees should consider retaining their discretion to reclaim bonuses if performance achievements are subsequently found to have been significantly mis-stated.

■ This latter point mirrors the debate on bonuses in the banking sector and is likely to remain an important issue – despite the legal difficulties that can arise when attempts to claw back payments are made.

■ If a service contract is to contain detailed provision about the calculation of the bonus, it will often be desirable to put this within a separate schedule. Such a schedule may specify:

– when the bonus is payable;

– whether the bonus is to be payable during part years when the director's employment has begun/ended and, if so, how any pro rata bonus payment is to be calculated;

– who is to decide the final figure;

– whether the bonus will always be payable on termination or only in certain circumstances;

– how particular terms such as 'net profits', etc are to be defined;

– whether the bonus forms part of pensionable earnings (the Corporate Governance Code recommends that it should not);

– whether there will be express performance criteria (as stated above, the Code recommends that there should be performance conditions and that they should be designed to enhance shareholder value);

– whether there will, in accordance with Code guidelines, be provision for a limit on the amount of bonus payable.

■ It may be sensible to have any detailed provision regarding bonus, including calculations derived from net profits, reviewed and approved by the company's auditors, particularly if the service contract will provide for reference to the auditors in the event of dispute.

Pensions

The service agreement must clearly provide for:

■ the director's entitlement to pension, subject to the rules of the scheme;

■ the employing company's entitlement to withdraw or amend the rules or benefits of a particular pension scheme and/or to terminate an individual's participation in it at any time. (Obviously, the director is likely to want assurance that, in the event of this type of provision being relied on, equivalent replacement benefits will be provided.)

In addition, provisions must reflect the tax treatment of pension contributions, which changed significantly in April 2006. (See Chapter 8.)

The issue of pension entitlement as part of a severance package hit the headlines (for all the wrong reasons) when the government bailed out Royal Bank of Scotland in 2008–09. The £700,000 a year package for departing chief executive Sir Fred Goodwin was roundly condemned as a reward for failure. (Sir Fred eventually bowed to public and political pressure and agreed in June 2009 to hand around £200,000 back.)

The Joint Statement suggests the following in relation to pensions:

Pension entitlement or contributions on severance can represent a large element of cost to shareholders. Remuneration committees should identify, review and disclose in the Remuneration Report any arrangements that guarantee pensions with limited or no abatement on severance or early retirement. These pension arrangements are no longer regarded as acceptable, except where they are generally available to all employees. Where opportunities arise, existing contracts should be amended. Such conditions should not be included in new contracts.

Permanent health insurance

Permanent health insurance (PHI) is designed to secure income for employees unable to work through sickness or injury. A PHI policy will usually be taken out by a company for a number of senior employees. The insurance provider will pay sums to the company after the employee has been ill for a specified period; payments will be made until the employee is able to return to work. A typical provision within a director's service contract may, therefore, entitle a director to six months' contractual sick pay and, thereafter, sums from the company as received under its PHI scheme.

While this is all very well in theory, in practice PHI can be a troublesome benefit. There is often a gulf between employees' perception of the scheme and the reality of how it operates.

A PHI policy will usually only provide cover for someone while they remain employed by the company. When an employee is dismissed because of long-term absence through illness (or for any other reason), their entitlement to PHI benefits automatically ceases. The understanding of employees, however, is often that PHI protects them against the impact of long-term illness and that they will continue to receive benefits for as long as they are ill – whether or not the employer chooses to dismiss them.

PHI entitlements have been the subject of a number of disputes. The leading case is that of Aspden v Webbs Poultry and Meat Group, in which it was held that an employee's contract contained an implied term that their employer would not dismiss them while sick if dismissal would lead to loss of entitlement to benefits under a PHI scheme.

The Aspden decision means that PHI provisions need very careful drafting and demand expert help. A common solution is for the contract to provide that:

■ the employing company will not terminate where an individual is absent through illness and is, or may become, entitled to PHI benefits;

■ the employing company will still be entitled to dismiss in certain specified circumstances – for example, gross misconduct, redundancy or where the individual ceases to be eligible for benefits under the PHI scheme.

Employers must make it expressly clear that an employee's entitlement to PHI is subject to the rules of the particular scheme. Failure to do so can be an expensive mistake: where the contractual promise exceeds the real levels of cover under the scheme the employer can find itself obliged to give benefits it will not be able to recover.

Share options

Provision for share options should not be made in a service agreement but in a separate side letter/agreement. This will ensure that:

■ the director's entitlement to share options depends entirely upon the provisions of the share option scheme;

■ the director will not be entitled to seek compensation for loss of share options as part of a wrongful dismissal claim.

6. Restrictive covenants

Purpose

The directors, as the most senior employees of a company, are likely to have strong relationships with the company's key customers, intimate knowledge of the company's most confidential information and, quite possibly, significant sway over the company's employees, many of whom they will probably have recruited. Given this, it is prudent for a company to protect itself against the risk of future competitive activity from a departing director. The mechanism for doing so is restrictive covenants.

There is an anecdotal view in some sectors that covenants are 'not worth the paper they are written on'. While it is true that justifying the need for and scope of covenants can be difficult, costing the company significant amounts in management time and legal fees, the UK courts do have a track record of enforcing appropriate and properly drafted restrictions.

Starting position of UK courts (restraint of trade doctrine)

A UK court will only enforce a particular covenant if:

■ it is satisfied, on reviewing the evidence, that the covenant is necessary to protect the company's legitimate business interests (historically, client connections, confidential information and workforce stability);

■ the particular covenant is drafted so as to provide the minimum necessary protection to those interests.

This reflects the need to protect and uphold the principle of free trade.

Ensuring enforceability

The key to enforceability is making sure that any covenant can be seen to have been tailored to the particular business of the company and the role that the employee will be carrying out. A long non-solicitation of customers covenant may be appropriate where a company has a limited number of important clients with whom it has developed a close relationship over time and from whom it receives instructions on a fairly infrequent basis – for example, once a year; it will be less easy to justify where a company has a significant number of more 'arm's length' customers who buy its products/services very frequently. Similarly, a 12-month non-solicitation restriction may be right for a sales director who has very close relationships with key customers and in-depth knowledge of their requirements but 'wrong' for a junior employee or a finance director who has no direct dealings with customers.

As a rule of thumb, courts will be reluctant to enforce employment covenants for more than a 12-month period. Six-month covenants will be easier to enforce, particularly in the case of non-compete restrictions (see below).

In cases where the departure of a director could be a real competitive threat to the business, detailed instructions should be given to a specialist employment lawyer so that covenants can be properly tailored and drafted.

Types of covenant

Non-compete covenants

These have often been viewed as unreasonable, extreme and, therefore, as difficult to enforce. A court will ask why sufficient protection to the business could not be provided by less stringent clauses (eg non-solicitation, non-dealing and non-poaching covenants or an express confidentiality provision) and will question the company's right to preclude an individual from joining a competitor.

It may, however, be possible to justify a non-compete provision where:

■ the company has a very local clientele that may be expected to follow a departing employee; thus, a hairdresser or estate agent may be justified in preventing someone from leaving and setting up in opposition in the same street;

■ the company can prove that significant technical or other business-critical information that is not necessarily client-specific and, therefore, not necessarily safeguarded by non-solicitation/dealing covenants, could not be adequately protected through an express confidentiality provision.

A 2007 decision by the Court of Appeal has confirmed that non-compete restrictions will be enforceable if drafted appropriately (see the following case notes box).

As stated above, the length of the restriction will be key. So, too, will its geographical scope: if a director has been primarily responsible for and had knowledge of a company's business in the south-east, a clause preventing them from competing anywhere in the United Kingdom is likely to be held to be too wide, and the court will not enforce it.

Case Notes: Thomas v Farr plc

In 2007, the Court of Appeal upheld a 12-month non-compete restriction for the former managing director of insurance broker Farr plc.

The managing director, Huw Thomas, had claimed the non-compete clause was an unreasonable restraint of trade and therefore unenforceable. But the court ruled that his position meant he was privy to commercially sensitive and strategic information that non-solicitation covenants and pure confidentiality provisions could not adequately protect.

The fact that it would be difficult for both employee and employer to draw the line between information that remained confidential post-termination and information that did not, only strengthened the argument, in the court's view, for a non-competition clause.

One of the keys to the ruling was the restriction's scope: Thomas was only prevented from competing in the sector that Farr specialised in – insurance for providers of social housing. He remained free to work in other areas of insurance, or to work in social housing insurance so long as he did not compete with Farr.

Finally, the court ruled that, since information about Farr's business could often remain confidential for more than 12 months, the duration of the restriction was also reasonable.

Non-solicitation covenants

The easiest type of covenant to enforce is usually that precluding an ex-director from soliciting his former employer's clients for a period following termination. Provided the length of the period is reasonable, and the covenant only covers the previous employer's line of business and those clients with whom the director has had individual dealings or of whom he has individual knowledge, a well-drafted non-solicitation of clients clause should be enforceable.

Non-dealing covenants

A non-dealing covenant not only precludes active solicitation of the former employer's clients but also acceptance of work from the former employer's clients – even when it is they who make the initial contact. Nonetheless, non-dealing restrictions can be enforceable. This is particularly true if the policing of a non-solicitation clause is likely to prove difficult.

Where non-solicitation and non-dealing restrictions are part of the same contract, they should be contained in 'severable' (ie separate) sub-clauses. This way, the employer will still be able to call on the non-solicitation clause if the non-dealing restriction is found to be too wide and, therefore, unenforceable.

In sectors where an employer may need to go through a lengthy tendering process for a contract or where the company invests heavily in building up contacts with potential clients, the company may wish to protect those potential leads as well as existing ones. The scope of non-solicitation and non-dealing covenants may thus extend beyond established customers.

Non-poaching covenants

The position on clauses to prevent a departing director recruiting former colleagues was in doubt for some years. Several cases have now made clear that, in the right circumstances, a UK court will enforce a non-poaching restriction.

The keys to enforceability are to ensure that the covenant:

■ is drafted only to cover those who may be expected to have particular knowledge of/influence with clients or knowledge of a company's confidential information;

■ is of reasonable duration.

Where a company is particularly concerned about the risk of poaching by a departing director it should consider further provisions. It could, for example:

■ expressly specify that information about employees' salaries and remuneration is confidential;

■ place directors and other senior employees under a contractual obligation to notify the company if a colleague or former colleague seeks to solicit them.

Non-interference with suppliers covenants

These covenants can be useful where a company is very reliant on relationships with certain key suppliers. They should be drafted to preclude interference with those relationships (and to make clear that they do not apply to the suppliers of general utilities).

Covenants and garden leave

Most companies will wish to protect themselves from competitive activity by a departing director not just through restrictive covenants but also through a 'garden leave' clause. On 'garden leave', an individual remains employed but is not given any duties. They serve out all or some of their notice at home, tending, the popular fiction is, to their garden.

Provided the clause is properly drafted, the individual will remain under a contractual and fiduciary obligation not to compete in any way with the company for the duration of the garden leave. Further restrictions will prohibit contact with customers or clients and deny access to offices, etc. The company therefore gets a breathing space – time to shore up customer contacts before the individual's departure.

The relationship between garden leave clauses and restrictive covenants has been a topic of debate. Should a company that wishes to rely on a restrictive covenant give credit for any period of garden leave? The leading case on the issue makes clear that this will not always be necessary. In practice, however, covenants are generally now drafted to apply for a particular period less any period of garden leave served.

Other related clauses

Well-drafted service agreements will contain various other provisions to make restrictive covenants more effective. They should, for example:

■ Allow the company to enforce restrictions on behalf of other group companies.

■ Oblige a director to make any prospective new employer aware of the terms of the restrictive covenants that apply to them (new employers who ignore the terms can be sued for inducing a breach of contract).

- Make clear that the director should not have any other business interests during the period of employment.

- Include an express confidentiality clause. Where particular categories of sensitive information exist, these should ideally be specified within the clause and be treated as confidential within the company.

Enforcement

The detail of how restrictive covenants may be enforced through an injunction or action for damages is beyond the scope of this text. The key point for a company that believes that an employee may have acted in breach of a covenant is to act quickly. Injunctions can prevent ex-employees and their new employers from taking certain steps but they are emergency measures; courts will be reluctant to grant them if they feel the company has been late in seeking relief.

7. Change of control/'golden parachute' clauses

Purpose

Change of control provisions entitle directors to enhanced severance packages in the event of companies being taken over or merged. They are known colloquially as 'golden parachute' clauses. A fairly typical feature of directors' service agreements in the 1980s, they became less common once the growing interest in corporate governance led to closer scrutiny of executives' contracts and of provisions for termination payments.

The usual justification for change of control clauses was that they provided security to directors who would not otherwise join or remain. Over time, however, this has lost credibility. The following arguments are likely to be made against change of control provisions:

- Directors' contracts often include long notice periods; these should be security enough. New owners of a company may lawfully terminate a director's employment without notice only if there are grounds for summary dismissal.

- Directors who are demoted after a takeover are protected by law: they can resign, claim constructive dismissal and seek damages consistent with their loss.

Enforceability

Code of directors' duties

To be justified, change of control provisions must be consistent with the code of directors' duties in the Companies Act 2006. As stated in Chapter 2, the code obliges directors to:

■ promote the success of the company;

■ act within their powers and use them for a proper purpose;

■ avoid putting themselves in a position where their personal interests conflict with their duties as a director.

If the provision for payment seems to be excessive and out of proportion with the benefit to the company, it can be challenged as a breach of these duties. The same applies if there is any evidence to suggest that the provision's primary purpose was to act as a 'poison pill' to deter a potential takeover bidder.

If the board and the remuneration committee believe that change of control provisions are necessary, it is advisable for them to minute the reasons why. They should be confident they can justify them as being consistent with the company's best interests; disclosure is likely to be necessary within the directors' remuneration report.

City Code on Takeovers and Mergers

Expert advice should be sought by any public company that wishes to consider amending directors' service agreements when there's a possible takeover.

The City Code on Takeovers and Mergers provides that companies that are the targets of bona fide offers, or that expect to be so imminently, must not enter into a contract 'otherwise than in the ordinary course of business' unless they have obtained the prior approval of shareholders in general meeting. It also says that:

> The Panel [on Takeovers and Mergers] will regard amending or entering into a service contract with, or creating or varying the terms of employment of, a director as entering into a contract 'otherwise than in the ordinary course of business'… if the new or amended contract or terms constitute an abnormal increase in the emoluments or a significant improvement in the terms of service. This will not prevent any increase or improvement which results from a genuine promotion or new appointment but the Panel must be consulted in advance in such cases.

The Takeover Code applies to all offers for companies whose shares are traded on a regulated market, and, thanks to the Companies Act 2006, now has a statutory basis.

Liquidated damages clauses and penalty clauses

Where advance provision is made for the damages payable to one party as a result of a breach of contract by the other, the courts will categorise the position in one of two ways. Liquidated damages clauses are those where the pre-estimate of loss is seen as being genuine; penalty clauses are those where it is not and where the sum stipulated is 'extravagant and unconscionable in comparison with the likely level of loss'. The former are, in principle, enforceable; the latter are void.

If a change of control clause is to be regarded as advance provision for damages, it will be necessary to demonstrate that it was framed on the basis of a genuine pre-estimate of loss. This will require evidence that proper consideration was given to an individual director's likely circumstances on termination and proper account was taken of their duty to mitigate their loss by seeking alternative employment.

There are those who say that change of control clauses should not be regarded as advance provision for damages payable as a result of a breach but as an express contractual provision under which the company/director is entitled to terminate the contract lawfully. While there is case law that supports this argument, the position is by no means certain. If a remuneration committee does decide that a change of control provision may be appropriate, it remains advisable for it to try to ensure that the amount of the proposed payment is a genuine pre-estimate of loss. This is also in a director's individual interests: it helps ensure that the change of control provision can, in due course, be relied upon.

The Joint Statement

The position of the ABI and NAPF on this issue is succinctly put:

> Contracts should not provide additional compensation for severance as a result of change of control.

8. Severance

The options

Dismiss summarily for gross misconduct

Where there is clear evidence of dishonesty or other serious misconduct amounting to a repudiatory breach, the company is legally entitled to dismiss the culprit with immediate effect, without any requirement to serve notice or pay in lieu of notice. The need for clear evidence, however, cannot be over-emphasised: in the majority of cases, instant dismissal carries a significant risk of litigation; there may be a High Court claim for wrongful dismissal and, possibly, a statutory claim for unfair dismissal, as discussed in section 9, page 138.

Serve notice and require director to work notice period

As stated in section 3, page 118, this option may not be in the best interests of the company. Directors who are asked to serve their full notice can be demotivated and even hostile towards the company and the remaining directors. Their main focus will, understandably, be on finding another job rather than ensuring the long-term success of the business. The company will usually prefer to cut ties – and bring in someone else – as soon as possible.

Serve notice and put on garden leave

Garden leave provisions are becoming increasingly common. The main reasons for this have been given in section 6, page 131. In summary: garden leave helps limit the threats to a business posed by a director's departure to a rival and can provide more security than covenants. It also gives the company time and space to negotiate a severance package.

The director on garden leave will often approach the company to agree an earlier termination date so that they can take up their new position. Their entitlement to further payment will then cease.

Garden leave is also useful where cash flow makes a lump sum payment in lieu undesirable.

Steps should be taken to ensure the terms of the garden leave are consistent with the director's contractual rights. The director should continue to receive all salary and benefits and should not be financially disadvantaged. An employing company should also ensure that there are very clear instructions about what a director can and cannot do while on garden leave. These should cover: contact with clients, employees or other business contacts; the steps the director is to take if contacted; the extent to which the director can be called upon to carry out particular tasks and provide assistance.

Terminate instantly under express payment in lieu provision

It is also increasingly common for service agreements to allow the company to terminate a director's employment on making a payment in lieu of notice. This provides a mechanism to bring the director's employment to an end instantly without being in breach of contract. Any restrictive covenants will continue to have effect insofar as they are enforceable. Further information about payment in lieu clauses appears in section 4, page 120.

Initiate a dialogue and negotiate a package

Frequently, the first instinct of the other directors/non-executive directors is to initiate a 'cards on the table' chat with a view to negotiating an appropriate package. This can work well, particularly if there is a good relationship between those who will have the discussion, the reasons for the departure are understood and the circumstances are not acrimonious – in other words, if the negotiations are likely to succeed.

But there are risks attached. Employment cases make clear that even where there is an agreement to talk off the record 'without prejudice', a party may still be able to rely on these discussions to support a legal claim. The risk is particularly acute where there has been no formal prior procedure. In these circumstances, the discussions and the absence of any formalities could be used in an unfair dismissal claim and/or negotiations for a significant sum in addition to contractual severance entitlements.

Legal and regulatory constraints

Sections 215 to 222 of the Companies Act 2006

The above sections preclude payments 'of compensation for loss of office' where particulars of the payment have not been approved by a company's shareholders. Generally, though, this will not apply. Section 220(1) of the Act provides for express exclusions in relation to a payment made in good faith:

■ in discharge of an existing legal obligation (effectively defined as an obligation that was not entered into in connection with or in consequence of the event giving rise to the payment);

■ by way of damages for breach of such an obligation;

■ by way of settlement or compromise of any claim arising in connection with the termination of the person's office or employment; or

■ by way of pension in respect of past services.

In addition, case law authority says that payments made to a departing director under express contractual provisions – for example, an express payment in lieu or golden parachute clause – are not covered by the requirement for shareholder approval. Sections 215 to 222 could be an issue, however, where a proposed payment to a director seems excessive in relation to their legal entitlements.

Code of directors' duties

If there is evidence to suggest that proposed payments are excessive when set against an individual director's legal entitlements, it's possible that the code of directors' duties has been breached and that the board's decision to authorise the payments could be challenged. The argument could be advanced that directors, in agreeing particular payments for a departing executive, were acting other than in the best interests of the company.

If a payment is proposed that seems out of line with an individual director's contractual entitlement and unfair dismissal rights, the company's remuneration committee or full board ought to minute the reasons why. Such payments will need to be justified.

The UK Corporate Governance Code

The Code (provision D.1.4) says that:

> The remuneration committee should carefully consider what compensation commitments (including pension contributions and all other elements) their directors' terms of appointment would entail in the event of early termination. The aim should be to avoid rewarding poor performance. They should take a robust line on reducing compensation to reflect departing directors' obligations to mitigate loss.

This provision can be useful when negotiating a package on behalf of a listed company. In particular, it can help endorse the point that payments must be closely linked to financial loss. If there is every reason to believe that a director with a 12 months' notice period would find a position within six months following termination, the remuneration committee would probably find a package of more than six months hard to justify to shareholders.

But 'avoiding rewarding poor performance' and 'taking a proper line to reflect mitigation' are often difficult to reconcile. A director employed under a contract with a 12 months' notice period is, in the absence of gross misconduct, entitled to 12 months' notice irrespective of performance. If they have performed poorly, it may be more difficult for them to find another job and thereby mitigate their loss. In other words, it can be more difficult to negotiate a discount when a director hasn't delivered.

Disclosure requirements

Full disclosure of amounts paid to departing directors is required in the directors' remuneration report, which, as explained in section 1, page 115, will be put to an advisory vote by shareholders. So a board needs to bear in mind the likely reaction of investors before any deal is agreed.

9. Potential legal claims

Wrongful dismissal

A wrongful dismissal is a dismissal that breaches the terms of the contract. If, therefore, a director is entitled to 12 months' notice but is dismissed instantly without notice, the company will be liable for damages; the director will be entitled to a payment equating to the loss of salary and benefits over the 12 months' notice period.

Any damages will, however, be subject to a reduction for mitigation. A dismissed employee is legally required to take reasonable steps to find an alternative job. If they succeed and take up a new position during the notice period, any sum earned will reduce the amount of their loss pound for pound. If a court is not satisfied that an employee has complied with the obligation to mitigate, this will be reflected in its award for compensation.

Successful wrongful dismissal claims prevent the employer from relying on any provisions within the contract: if the employer is held to have breached the contract, it cannot enforce terms such as restrictive covenants, and these will consequently fall away. It is largely because of this that, where restrictive covenants exist, it is now standard practice to add a contractual payment in lieu provision allowing the company to terminate instantly without breaching the contract.

Unfair dismissal

Every person in Great Britain who has been employed for one year or more has a statutory right not to be unfairly dismissed. This right applies just as much to an employed director as to any other employee. Dismissal will only be found to be fair if:

- it is made for a potentially fair reason, such as redundancy, poor performance or poor conduct;

- before dismissing or serving notice, the employer followed the necessary fair procedure (see below);

- it is reasonable to dismiss in all the circumstances of the case.

Until quite recently, unfair dismissal was not a significant factor in the majority of cases relating to the termination of directors' contracts. This was because compensation for unfair dismissal was limited when set against a director's contractual entitlement. The potential compensation recoverable for unfair dismissal has now, however, significantly increased. In addition to a basic award (which is still a limited amount, calculated in the same way as a statutory redundancy payment), an employee who has been unfairly dismissed is entitled to a compensatory award (dependent on their losses), the statutory maximum for which is now £65,300.

A further significant change took place in 2004. New statutory disciplinary and grievance procedures were introduced, requiring an employer to go through a minimum disciplinary procedure before dismissing someone. The procedure included:

- calling the employee to attend a disciplinary hearing;

- providing the employee with details of matters to be discussed before the hearing;

- notifying the employee of the decision made after the hearing and providing the right to appeal.

If these minimum procedures were not followed, the dismissal was automatically deemed to be unfair and the compensation awarded could be subject to an uplift of between 10 and 50 per cent.

The good news for companies is that the statutory procedures were repealed with effect from 6 April 2009. In their place is a new Code of Practice on disciplinary and grievance procedures from the Advisory, Conciliation and Arbitration Service (ACAS). The Code sets out minimum standards for dealing with disciplinary matters, but there is no longer a requirement to follow a mandatory dispute resolution procedure in advance of dismissal and no automatic unfairness when the Code is not followed.

What does this mean in practice? The ACAS Code is not legally binding, but when deciding if a dismissal was fair or not, an employment tribunal will look at whether the Code was followed. If an employment tribunal decides that an employer failed to follow the Code and that was unreasonable, it may increase the compensation awarded by up to 25 per cent.

The appropriateness of unfair dismissal claims will, of course, vary. A director is not entitled to double recovery in relation to the same period of loss. This means, for example, that if a director is being paid in lieu of a 12-month notice period (either under an express clause or as a result of reaching agreement to make a payment in lieu) and they can mitigate their losses within the 12 months by finding another position, legal action will, from a practical point of view, be irrelevant. The director could seek to recover a basic award but this will be little more than a nominal sum. As regards the compensatory award, the director will not be able to demonstrate any losses: they will have been more than compensated by the payment in lieu.

If, on the other hand, a director's actual losses are likely to exceed payments made under their contractual entitlements, an unfair dismissal claim becomes much more relevant. In these circumstances, an employing company that has failed to go through a fair procedure before giving notice could be in trouble. To avoid the risk of litigation, it will need to:

■ increase the proposed severance package by a sum that exceeds contractual entitlements and reflects the amount that could be paid in unfair dismissal compensation;

■ get the director to sign a compromise agreement that prohibits any claim.

Other

This section has dealt with the most likely actions when a company dismisses a director. It is important to remember, though, that others could arise – for example, the claim that a director's dismissal was on discriminatory grounds.

7

Remuneration Issues

As will be clear from the previous chapter, decisions on the remuneration of directors cannot be made in a vacuum. Employers must take into account not only what competitors and comparable companies do but also what the government, shareholders and the public expect. Stark reminders of this were given in 2009 when news of the retirement package awarded to Sir Fred Goodwin, former chief executive of Royal Bank of Scotland, met a storm of protest.

Pay policies must not only attract and retain the best executive talent, but also be fair and justifiable.

This chapter aims to give a guide not only to the practical components of executive pay and rewards but also to the development of good remuneration policies and the practices that will win the support of investors. It examines some of the challenges companies face when trying to devise packages that are both cost-effective and 'efficient' and that conform to best practice. And it looks at trends likely to influence executive remuneration in the future.

1. The post credit-crunch outlook

The demands on companies setting remuneration policy have, arguably, never been greater.

As Sir Fred Goodwin discovered, the 2008 financial crisis and the subsequent recession created a flashpoint. Tolerance of 'rewards for failure', excessive bonuses and of any elements of remuneration that couldn't be justified by overall company performance hit an all-time low. In

2009, shareholders, increasingly vocal on the subject of pay, voted against remuneration reports at several AGMs (see the box on investor activism, below) and staged significant rebellions at others.

The same year, the government promised to implement a recommendation of the Walker Report (see the box on governance initiatives, page 143) in the Financial Services Bill, forcing banks and other large financial institutions to make disclosures on the pay of their high-earning employees.

Meanwhile, companies were having to get to grips with changes to the tax regime for high earners, effective from April 2010. The first increases to the top rate of income tax in over 20 years (allied to restrictions on income tax relief for pension contributions) caused many employers to look at how they reward executives. Compensating for higher tax rates by increasing pay packages is very much frowned on, but changes to the tax system always encourage employers to explore ways to deliver existing benefits more efficiently. In December 2009, the ABI warned against pursuing greater tax efficiency in pay if it meant increased costs for the company.

Investor Activism

Shareholder activism has, over recent years, been positively encouraged by the government. Since 2003, investors in listed companies have been entitled to an advisory vote on a report detailing directors' remuneration. A vote against has no legal effect, but it does send a strong signal of shareholder discontent and, in the recessionary climate of 2009, activism hit new levels. Five companies had their directors' remuneration reports 'thrown out' and several others, BP among them, came close to losing the vote.

The most spectacular rebellion took place at the April AGM of Royal Bank of Scotland, bailed out by the taxpayer the previous year. The company's remuneration report was rejected by more than 90 per cent of the votes cast, with the UK Treasury adding its own 70 per cent shareholding to the cause.

Given the pension awarded to Sir Fred Goodwin, former chief executive of RBS, and the part played by banks in the financial crisis, the 'no' vote was hardly a surprise. But anger, in 2009, was not reserved for the financial services sector. The remuneration policies of all listed companies were under close scrutiny from institutional investors.

Peter Montagnon, the director of investment affairs at the ABI, gave companies some warning of what to expect at the start of the year when he said: 'You would be foolish to delude yourself that if you are paying out bonuses in bad times then people aren't going to notice.'

The first company to have its remuneration report defeated in 2009 was not a bank but a house builder. Bellway plc changed the performance targets it had previously told investors it would use. Bonuses were paid not on the basis of operating profits but of new cash management and debt reduction targets introduced during the course of the previous financial year. To the ABI it seemed obvious that targets had been abandoned when it became clear they weren't going to be met. Fifty nine per cent of shareholders voted against the remuneration report, making clear their disapproval of remuneration committees that exercise a discretion to change previously disclosed performance conditions. The board later admitted it was wrong not to have consulted major shareholders earlier.

Five months later, in May 2009, blue-chip company Shell found itself in similar trouble. This time, investors focused on the use of a remuneration committee discretion that allowed pay-outs under a long-term incentive plan. Shell had narrowly failed to meet its comparative TSR target (third place for total shareholder return measured against a small group of five global oil companies), but the remuneration committee nonetheless allowed 50 per cent of awards to vest, justifying its decision on the basis of the company's consistently strong financial performance. The TSR target had only just been missed, but the remuneration report was rejected by nearly 60 per cent of the votes cast.

Governance Initiatives

Boardroom pay has long been a contentious issue, with stories of 'fat cats' and 'rewards for failure' regularly on the front pages and prompting initiatives from both Conservative and Labour governments.

The debate was never more fierce than in 2008, when the Financial Services Authority (FSA) and the Treasury Select Committee (among others) claimed pay structures (particularly bonuses) had contributed to a culture of excessive risk-taking among Britain's banks, thereby helping to precipitate a major economic crisis.

The result was a number of further initiatives to improve

corporate governance and reform remuneration practices; 2009 saw the publication of:

- the FSA's Remuneration Code, requiring the United Kingdom's largest financial institutions to 'establish, implement and maintain policies, procedures and practices that are consistent with and promote effective risk management';

- the Walker Report on the corporate governance of the financial services sector;

- a revised UK Corporate Governance Code from the Financial Reporting Council (FRC) – see Chapter 4.

In August 2009, 26 of the UK's largest financial institutions (banks, broker-dealers and certain building societies) became subject to the FSA's Remuneration Code and will be expected to follow at least some of the Walker rules on pay, a summary of which is given below.

- The remuneration committee should be directly responsible for the pay of not just directors but also of those regarded by the FSA as having a 'significant influence function' or who may have 'a material impact on the risk profile of the entity'. This will give the committee a greater control over a company's pay practices.

- In addition, the remuneration committee should have oversight of remuneration policy throughout the business, though it will only set pay packages for the most senior staff.

- The remuneration committee should confirm, in its report, that it is satisfied with the way that performance objectives and risk adjustments are reflected in compensation structures for senior management.

- It must also report whether it has the power to enhance an executive's benefits in certain circumstances such as termination of employment or a change of control.

- Banks should disclose the number (but not the names) of employees earning more than £1m, broken down into bands of pay.

- At least half of an executive's incentive pay should be in the form of a long-term incentive scheme with performance conditions, and with half the award vesting after three years and the rest after five years.

- ■ Two-thirds of cash bonuses should be deferred and paid over the two years following the performance year.

- ■ Clawback should apply in the event of mis-statement or misconduct.

- ■ The chairman of the remco should face re-election at the following year's AGM if the remuneration report receives less than 75 per cent approval.

- ■ There should be a Remuneration Consultants Code of best practice for those who advise boards on executive pay.

The Walker Report did not just have an impact on the banks and large financial institutions it was aimed at. The FRC adopted some of its recommendations for all listed companies in a new UK Corporate Governance Code that includes the following:

- ■ a supporting principle on the need for performance-related remuneration to be aligned with the long-term success of the company;

- ■ references to the link between remuneration and risk policy, to the use of non-financial metrics when measuring performance and to arrangements for reclaiming variable components of pay if circumstances demand it;

- ■ provisions to discourage all forms of performance-related remuneration for non-executive directors, not just share options.

2. Reference points

The legal and regulatory framework for executive remuneration is outlined in section 1 of the previous chapter. Employers in general – and quoted companies in particular – should pay particular attention to:

- ■ Section D (remuneration) and Schedule A (provisions on the design of performance-related remuneration) of the **UK Corporate Governance Code**;

- ■ LR 9.8.8 (relating to disclosure of directors' remuneration) and LR 9.4 and LR 13.8.11 to 13.8.15 (relating to approval of share plans by shareholders) of the **Financial Services Authority's Listing Rules**;

■ **Regulations under the Companies Act 2006** that prescribe the content of the directors' remuneration report for listed companies and set out the basic remuneration disclosure requirements for all companies;

■ **the guidelines of UK institutional investor bodies**, especially those of the Association of British Insurers or ABI ('Executive Remuneration – ABI Guidelines on Policies and Practices') and of RiskMetrics, an independent governance body, but one that retains strong links with the National Association of Pension Funds (NAPF).

3. Remuneration and unquoted companies

The main focus of this chapter is quoted companies and, principally, fully listed companies rather than those with shares traded on the Alternative Investment Market (AIM).

However, some of the issues covered will be common to all companies. What level of shareholder dilution is acceptable for share plans? What should annual bonus performance targets be? These questions can be universal.

Also, the system and procedures for deciding remuneration can be the same in a private company as they are in a public one. An unquoted company, may, for example, set up a separate remuneration committee involving non-executive directors. In some cases, the practice will be imported by investors and non-executives who join the business from a public-company background. In others, it will result from a desire to demonstrate good governance practice to potential outside investors.

The position of AIM companies is illustrative. AIM companies are not listed companies for these purposes, and therefore do not have to comply with the disclosure requirements for listed companies' remuneration reports or to put such reports to a vote of shareholders; AIM companies are not subject to the Corporate Governance Code; the AIM rules do not require companies to seek shareholders' approval to establish new share plans. However, many AIM companies:

■ make much fuller disclosure on remuneration than is required under the Companies Act and will produce a separate remuneration report within their annual report and accounts;

■ voluntarily adopt some of the Corporate Governance Code's recommendations, having, for example, remuneration committees made up of independent non-executives;

■ frequently model their share plans on share plans for fully listed companies, particularly with regard to performance conditions, dilution capacity, limits on individual awards and the requirement to seek shareholders' approval for changes that benefit participants.

Under new rules for AIM companies with accounting periods ending on or after 31 March 2010, they will have to disclose in their accounts the emoluments and compensation paid to each director, benefits under share plans and company contributions to their pension.

4. Deciding remuneration packages

Best practice; the remuneration committee

Principle D.2 of the UK Corporate Governance Code states that:

There should be a formal and transparent procedure for developing policy on executive remuneration and for fixing the remuneration packages of individual directors. No director should be involved in deciding his or her own remuneration.

Listed companies fulfil this obligation by having a remuneration committee.

Committee membership

According to provision D.2.1 of the Code, remuneration committees should comprise 'at least three, or in the case of smaller companies two, independent non-executive directors'.

A smaller company is a company outside the FTSE 350. The Code's tests of 'independence' are discussed in Chapter 4 on corporate governance.

In addition, the company chairman may sit on, but not chair, the remuneration committee if he or she was considered independent on appointment as chairman.

The committee's terms of reference

Remuneration committees must, says the Code, make their terms of reference publicly available – an obligation usually fulfilled via the company's website. The Institute of Chartered Secretaries and Administrators (ICSA) has published guidance notes giving model terms of reference. These can be downloaded from its website.

Central to the role of the 'remco' is the concept of delegated responsibility. The terms of reference must make clear that committee members actually set the remuneration for all executive directors and the chairman; their role is not merely to make suggestions.

Furthermore, the influence of the committee extends beyond the pay of the boardroom. Code provision D.2.2. says:

> The committee should also recommend and monitor the level and structure of remuneration for senior management.

The Code's expectation is that 'senior management' should normally include the first layer of management below board level.

The Walker Report has added to the remuneration committee's responsibilities for pay outside the boardroom in the case of banks and other financial institutions – see the box on pages 143–45.

Appointment of remuneration consultants

The Corporate Governance Code (supporting principle D.2) says that remuneration committees should be responsible for any appointment of consultants 'in respect of executive director remuneration'. It also says (D.2.1) that the company must state publicly (again via its website) whether the appointed consultants have any other connections with the company.

These points are echoed in – and given more force by – regulations made under the Companies Act, which require the committee to disclose in the remuneration report:

■ the name of any person who assisted it in the consideration of any matter (this applies not only to external advisers but also to internal company officers such as senior HR executives);

■ whether that person provided any other services to the company during the relevant financial year;

■ whether that person was appointed by the committee.

The Walker Report has promoted a 'Code of Conduct' for remuneration consultants aimed at minimising potential conflicts of interest.

5. Institutional investors

The ABI and the NAPF

'Executive Remuneration – ABI Guidelines on Policies and Practices' reflects the views of members of the ABI on features of remuneration practice.

The guidelines generally provide a good insight into views among institutional investors on remuneration matters. They are usually updated each year, but, mindful of inducing 'change fatigue', few amendments have been made since they were substantially re-styled in December 2006. The current format of the guidelines mirrors that of the Corporate Governance Code (see the box on page 150).

The ABI also runs a comprehensive monitoring service – the Institutional Voting Information Service (IVIS) – that is widely used by institutional investors. IVIS reviews the remuneration reports and AGM proposals for share plans of every FTSE All-Share company and produces a report that is available to subscribers. It also reports on general Code compliance.

IVIS operates a colour-coding system for companies:

- **blue top** – complies with ABI guidelines and corporate governance best practice;

- **amber top** – gives cause for concern;

- **red top** – non-compliant or inconsistent with guidelines, resulting in a decision by members to abstain or vote against;

- **green top** – previously reported as inconsistent or non-compliant but the problem is now resolved.

The NAPF is also an important and influential body. Although it no longer runs a service such as IVIS, it retains links to RiskMetrics, the UK arm of proxy voting information service, Institutional Shareholder Services (ISS).

ISS's recommendations are widely followed by US institutional investors. Consequently, a favourable report from RiskMetrics will be important in securing the support of any US institutional investors for remuneration report votes or AGM share plan proposals.

RiskMetrics also produces its own 'Corporate Governance Policy'. In places, this has a different emphasis from the ABI's guidelines.

PIRC

A further monitoring service on governance and remuneration matters is provided by Pensions and Investment Research Consultants (PIRC).

PIRC is an independent organisation, but its reports are taken by a number of institutional investors and its recommendations frequently attract press attention. The service is designed to help institutional investors make 'considered use' of their votes.

The ABI's Guidelines

In response to criticism that its guidelines had become impenetrable for companies and were essentially a 'practitioners' document', the ABI substantially re-styled them in December 2006. The current format features:

■ five key principles;

■ 17 main provisions; and

■ detailed guidance supporting the 17 main provisions.

The five key principles are set out below.

■ Boards are responsible for adopting remuneration policies and practices that promote the success of companies in creating value for shareholders over the longer term. The policies and practices should be demonstrably aligned with the corporate objectives and business strategy, taking risks fully into account and reviewed regularly.

■ Remuneration committees should be established in accordance with the provisions of the UK Corporate Governance Code. They should comprise independent directors who bring thought and scrutiny to all aspects of remuneration. It is important to maintain a constructive and timely dialogue between boards and shareholders regarding remuneration policies and practices.

■ Executive remuneration should be set at levels that retain and motivate, based on selection and interpretation of appropriate benchmarks. Such benchmarks should be used with caution, in view of the risk of an upward ratcheting of remuneration levels with no corresponding improvement in performance.

■ Executive remuneration should be linked to individual and corporate performance through graduated targets, which align the interests of executives with those of shareholders. The resulting arrangements should be clear and readily understandable.

■ Shareholders will not support arrangements that entitle executives to reward when this is not justified by performance. Remuneration committees should ensure that service contracts contain provisions that are consistent with this principle.

Individual institutions

Individual institutions tend to have marked preferences in relation to certain aspects of remuneration practice. For example, some greatly prefer one form of performance condition for long-term incentives to another.

This means that it is often not enough to talk to a representative body when trying to establish your shareholders' views on remuneration, or simply to refer to published ABI and NAPF guidelines. In many cases, you need also to approach the individual corporate governance officers at the relevant institutions.

Consultation

ABI guidelines give a very clear endorsement to the practice of informally consulting shareholders about any proposed changes to a company's remuneration practice.

The following box gives further information on how the process of informal consultation usually works.

Consulting Institutional Shareholders: a Brief Guide

Timing – the consultation should normally take place in advance of the publication of a remuneration report and/or AGM shareholders' circular in which a company would be required to set out its proposals formally. This gives institutions an opportunity to comment on proposals and (if appropriate) for the company to make any modifications to secure shareholder support.

Method – the process should be initiated by the company (normally in the shape of the remuneration committee chairman) writing to major shareholders. The letter will outline the main aspects of the proposals (for example, performance conditions, dilution impacts, the level of individual awards). The letter should set a deadline for responses and also give contact points for queries – the remuneration committee chairman, a company officer familiar with the proposals such as the company secretary or, sometimes, an external adviser. Some consultations can be more intensive and involve a 'roadshow' presentation for investors.

Scope – cases vary, but companies typically consult their leading 10 or so institutional investors, and any other investors that they regard as having an interest above a significant threshold (eg one per cent or 1.5 per cent of issued share capital). In addition, a company should probably include any investors who have previously commented on the company's remuneration practices, even if they are outside the parameters set for the consultation. Companies will also generally consult the ABI and RiskMetrics or at least make them aware that a consultation with individual investors is in progress.

The ABI may itself play an important role in the exercise – through giving its own views on proposals and (when asked to do so) through coordinating the responses of interested ABI members.

6. Design of remuneration packages

This section considers some of the approaches companies take to the design of base salary, benefits, annual bonuses and pensions. Share incentives are considered in the next section.

'Total remuneration' and the 'balance' of the package

Many companies look at packages on a 'total remuneration' basis – that is, they consider all the elements of an executive's package together, rather than each one (base salary, benefits, pension entitlements, annual bonus and share incentives) in isolation.

In theory, this allows them to compare the 'total value' of remuneration packages in their sector or market. But, while useful, a total remuneration analysis can only be an approximate guide. The differences between the separate elements of remuneration packages can make like-for-like comparisons difficult. One company may, for example, offer an expensive final salary pension plan; another, a money purchase plan.

An alternative approach is to focus on the 'balance' within a package between the fixed elements (base salary, benefits, pensions) and the variable or performance-linked elements (annual bonus, share incentives). The balance of a package is given emphasis in both the Corporate Governance Code and the ABI guidelines.

Principle D.1 of the Code states:

Levels of remuneration should be sufficient to attract, retain and motivate directors of the quality required to run the company successfully, but a company should avoid paying more than is necessary for this purpose. A significant proportion of executive directors' remuneration should be structured so as to link rewards to corporate and individual performance.

The ABI's guidelines for the structure of remuneration say:

> Remuneration committees are responsible for ensuring that the mix of incentives reflects the company's needs, establishes an appropriate balance between fixed and variable remuneration, and is based on targets that are appropriately stretching, verifiable and relevant and which take account of risk.

Whatever the balance, the government wants the details to be disclosed. Regulations under the Companies Act require a listed company to disclose the relative importance of performance-linked and non-performance-linked elements of remuneration. Many companies fulfil this requirement by including in the policy section of their remuneration report a form of 'boilerplate' that tracks the wording of the Code closely – for example: 'a significant proportion of directors' remuneration is performance-linked through participation in the annual bonus plan and share incentive plans'. Others go further, using graphs to illustrate the relative importance of the elements of a director's remuneration. An example would be a bar chart showing a split between salary (40 per cent), target annual bonus (30 per cent) and expected long-term share incentives (30 per cent).

Base salary

Base salary remains the foundation stone of remuneration packages, often determining the levels of other elements such as pensions and bonuses.

When setting base salaries for executive directors, companies typically bear in mind:

- the director's performance, individual responsibilities and experience;
- comparisons with salary levels in other companies.

The former is the more important criterion. While external comparisons can be a useful 'benchmark', they should never be used as the sole justification for salary levels. Indeed, the 'bandwagon' argument will always be difficult to sell to investors. This is evident from the Corporate Governance Code, where the supporting principle to D1 says:

The remuneration committee should judge where to position their company relative to other companies. But they should use such comparisons with caution, in view of the risk of an upward ratchet of remuneration levels with no corresponding improvement in performance.

This statement has been followed in the ABI's 'Key Principles' (see the box on page 149).

When looking at salary data, remuneration committees should ask:

■ How appropriate are the comparator companies? Should a broader cross-sectoral group of companies with similar market capitalisation and turnover be considered as a 'health-check'?

■ How large is the salary comparator group? Could removing or adding, say, one or two companies significantly alter a quartile analysis?

■ How up-to-date is the data? Could there have been intervening salary reviews? Has the data been 'aged' to reflect possible earnings inflation? Is the ageing factor appropriate?

In 2009, virtually any significant rise in base pay was criticised by institutional investors, and many companies were reported as freezing directors' salary levels.

Benefits

With the exception of permanent health insurance (see page 126), benefits are typically non-contentious. They will usually comprise a mix of insurance benefits and fringe elements or perquisites such as cars and other extras.

Changes to the tax system have led companies to review their approach to benefits. Some now offer a flexible programme whereby employees can choose the things they want from a benefits 'menu' – provided, of course, they stick to a budget.

Annual bonus

The Corporate Governance Code's guidance on the design of annual bonus plans is set out in Schedule A, paragraph 1:

The remuneration committee should consider whether the directors should be eligible for annual bonuses. If so, performance conditions should be relevant, stretching and designed to enhance shareholder value and to promote the long-term success of the company. Upper limits should be set and disclosed. There may be a case for part payment in shares to be held for a significant period.

Typical features of annual bonus plans include:

- **performance targets** based on internal financial measures (for example, budgeted profits before tax, sales or economic value added), company development measures (for example, product development goals) or personal performance measures (for example, employee safety records);

- **payments linked to performance targets** – with the maximum paid for achievement that exceeds budgeted or predicted levels to a degree specified by the remuneration committee.

Where executives have group-wide responsibilities, the performance targets are likely to focus on group performance. Where executives have distinct divisional responsibilities, the targets will usually include some weighting towards divisional performance.

The amount of bonus payable for achieving budgeted or target levels of performance can vary significantly from company to company; it will depend on how stretching the remuneration committee thinks the initial budgeted targets are. For example, some annual bonus plans are structured so that payments are heavily weighted towards achieving the budgeted targets or better. Around half of the maximum may be payable for achieving the budgeted target and only a low level (for example, 10 per cent of the maximum) for near achievement (say, 90 per cent or 95 per cent) of budgeted targets.

Deferral of part or all of a bonus into shares is becoming increasingly common. It is seen by shareholders as a way of aligning directors' interests with theirs; if part of the bonus is delivered in shares after, say, two or three years, the director has a good reason to stay with the company and to improve shareholder returns. (The shares will usually be forfeited if the director leaves during the deferral period.)

This trend is likely to develop further, particularly among larger companies. The Walker guidelines endorse deferral of annual bonus, calling it 'the primary risk-adjustment mechanism' for annual bonus. Additionally, they recommend a deferral of two-thirds of annual bonus into shares for a three-year period.

Unlike long-term share incentive schemes, deferred bonus plans for directors do not need shareholder approval under the Listing Rules, provided they do not involve the issue of new shares.

Companies also get off fairly lightly when it comes to the disclosure rules for bonuses. They must disclose in their annual report and accounts:

- any bonuses paid in respect of the financial year;

- the bonus maximum for the current financial year.

Other than that, there are no formal requirements – largely because disclosures of performance conditions based on internal budgets could involve the release of commercially sensitive information.

However, institutional investors have made a concerted push for more disclosure in relation to annual bonuses in recent years. Investors would prefer to see:

■ for the most recent year's bonus, full retrospective disclosure of any financial targets and the company's performance against them, leading to the calculation of bonus earned;

■ for the most recent year's bonus, details of any personal performance metrics;

■ for a current year's bonus, a description of the performance metrics to be applied – without the disclosure of commercially sensitive numbers.

Investors are keen to see that personal performance measures are real and quantifiable and not a way of making a purely discretionary award.

Pensions

The nature and potential cost of executive directors' pensions has long been keeping finance directors awake at night. This is not just because of the much publicised and continuing 'pensions crisis'.

Company law requirements for the disclosure of the total transfer value of an individual director's pension raised the prospect of a media frenzy, with large numbers providing an easy target for journalists. Companies' fears, though, have not been realised. This is probably for two reasons:

■ pensions disclosures are difficult to understand and to value, particularly on a comparative basis;

■ there is greater understanding that pensions often represent long-standing contractual promises (particularly in respect of older final salary plans).

Restrictions on income-tax relief for pension contributions mean the practice of paying executives a fully-taxable 'pension replacement' cash sum, in lieu of an actual pension contribution, is likely to continue.

Such supplements are often lower than the pension contributions they replace. This is due to the additional employers' National Insurance cost on the cash payments: the company indirectly passes this to the director by scaling down the salary supplement.

More detailed information on pensions and the current tax regime is given in Chapter 8.

Rewarding Non-executive Directors

The Walker Report and the UK Corporate Governance Code emphasise the need for non-executives to have sufficient time to devote to their increased responsibilities (see Chapter 4); and investor and media focus on the role of non-executives in protecting shareholders' interests further increases the burdens.

So how should companies decide NEDs' fees?

The key determinants

Levels of remuneration for non-executive directors should reflect the time commitment and responsibilities of the role – provision D.1.3 of the Corporate Governance Code.

Many companies accordingly break NEDs' fees down into:

■ a basic fee;

■ additional fees for committee membership (eg remuneration or nomination committee);

■ further fees for the responsibility of chairing a committee.

In line with the Smith guidance (annexed to the Code), companies should consider paying a premium for membership and chairmanship of the audit committee.

If companies benchmark their NEDs' fees against those paid by other companies, they will typically look at companies where non-executives have comparable time commitments. Survey data on NEDs' fees is differentiated on this basis.

Other considerations

Articles of association

As noted in Chapter 6 (section 5), a company's articles may limit the amount the company can pay in directors' fees. NEDs' fees will count towards this limit, and the articles should therefore be checked when additional non-executives are appointed or when fees are reviewed.

Shares, share options and performance-related pay

The Corporate Governance Code and the ABI and RiskMetrics guidelines are all strongly against participation by non-executives in **share options or other performance-related pay**. The rationale for this is that such remuneration will compromise a non-executive director's independence.

However, some companies will pay all or part of the fees in shares. The ABI guidelines encourage non-executives to use their fees to acquire shares in the company as this is seen as promoting alignment with shareholders.

---

7. Design of share incentive plans

This section considers some of the key issues for companies when designing share incentive plans. It describes the different types of plans and performance conditions and looks at their advantages and disadvantages.

Background

Share plans differ from other parts of the remuneration package in several important respects.

Under the Listing Rules, a share plan will require shareholders' approval if:

■ it may involve the issue of new shares (or transfer of treasury shares) by the company;

■ it is a 'long-term incentive scheme' (ie it is conditional on service and/or performance over more than one financial year) in which the directors can participate.

Institutional shareholders publish specific and detailed guidelines for share incentive plans. This is not just because of the requirement for shareholder approval. Certain aspects of the plans will materially affect their interests: issues of new shares will involve direct dilution of their holdings.

Share incentives deliver rewards if disclosable performance conditions are met. Accordingly, shareholders focus on whether such conditions are, in their view, sufficiently demanding.

Design issues

(i) Motivation and retention

To serve their commercial purposes – ie to achieve and sustain improvements in performance and increase the commitment of individuals to the business and its goals – plans must be valued by participants.

So both plan design and choice of performance conditions are crucial. A clear 'line of sight' between performance conditions and rewards will serve the interests of both companies and their shareholders.

Where companies step back and ask 'is our plan working?', the answer can result in a bespoke solution. An example is the approach taken by Venture, now part of Centrica, to the design of its long-term incentive plan in 2008 (see the following box).

Innovative Design: Venture Production plc

As an oil production company, Venture, now owned by the Centrica group, took the view that profits-based measures were not the way to align managers' interests with the strategic goals of the business. Profits could go up or down depending on factors that were outside managers' control – particularly, the price of oil.

In 2008, therefore, the company chose production as one of its performance measures. Under its long-term incentive plan:

- ■ one-third of awards were dependent on actual oil production targets;
- ■ one-third on proven or probable oil reserve targets;
- ■ one-third on annual growth in total shareholder return (TSR).

Awards would normally vest after four years, with the possibility of early vesting after three years if one of the oil production targets and an average TSR growth of 20 per cent a year were achieved.

(ii) Revised accounting treatment of share incentives

The introduction of the international accounting standard IFRS 2 on 1 January 2005 significantly changed the accounting rules for share-based payments. For listed companies, an 'expected value' charge must be taken to the profit and loss account for all forms of share incentives. This rule has also applied to AIM companies since 1 January 2006.

The effect has been to alter significantly the previous distinction between share options with a market value 'exercise price', which had no profit and loss impact where new-issue shares were involved, and share plans that delivered 'free shares', where there was a profit and loss charge based broadly on the value of the underlying shares at the time an award was granted.

Put simply, share options are not cost free in accounting terms. Consequently, many companies have considered whether alternative plans may have more potential to deliver rewards for comparable profit and loss costs. This thinking has led to the predominance of Preference Share Plans or 'LTIPs' among quoted companies (see table, page 162).

(iii) Dilution pressures

Companies have to abide by the restrictions agreed with shareholders on the number of new shares they can issue under share plans. The long-standing limits contained in the ABI's guidelines mean that:

■ shares equal to no more than 10 per cent of issued share capital are available to be issued as awards under share plans in any 10-year period;

■ shares equal to no more than five per cent of issued share capital are available to be issued as awards made under discretionary or 'executive' share plans in any 10-year period.

(iv) Views of institutional investors

As stated earlier, institutional investors pay close attention to the performance conditions that companies apply to share incentives. This has resulted in the following developments:

■ a range and 'sliding scale' of performance targets, with full vesting conditional on the attainment of the highest, and only a proportion (for example, 25 per cent) vesting for the lowest;

■ the removal of re-testing of performance conditions, so that if a condition is not met over an initial period the award lapses;

■ where companies propose earnings per share (EPS) targets, investors will compare these with consensus brokers' forecasts to determine whether the conditions are sufficiently 'stretching';

■ a focus on the size and composition of groups of comparator companies selected for total shareholder return (TSR) targets.

Main types of share incentive plan

There are three main types of share incentive plan currently used by UK companies.

(i) Share options

Share options have been a popular way to motivate employees. They have several advantages:

- they are straightforward and generally easily understood by participants;

- they mean the interests of employees and shareholders are aligned – participants will want to see continued rises in the company's share price;

- up to £30,000-worth of HM Revenue & Customs approved options per employee are treated as capital gains rather than income for tax purposes and escape National Insurance. (Additionally, companies whose gross assets are less than £30m can benefit from the highly tax efficient Enterprise Management Incentive plans.)

Nonetheless, many quoted companies have chosen to review their share option plans. This is not just because of the accounting changes outlined earlier. Other factors are involved. Share options:

- may not provide an adequate reward or retention mechanism in a sustained bear market;

- can use up a company's available dilution limits (because the advantage for the employee is the rise in the share price, the number of shares needed to provide a significant benefit can be large);

- are subject to tough performance conditions at the insistence of institutional investors.

(ii) Performance Share Plans (PSPs)

Under a PSP, an executive is granted free shares – provided the company's performance meets a set target, or targets, over a subsequent period (usually three years).

The previous accounting treatment of share awards involved a profit and loss expense to the company in the case of PSPs. With the introduction of IFRS 2 (see page 159), this distinction between PSPs and market value options has been lessened and the relative profit and loss costs of PSPs and share options can now be compared.

The main advantages of PSPs are that:

- awards retain their value in a bear market and continue to be a useful reward and retention tool;

- they can allow for a closer connection between individual management performance and reward than share options, where the main driver of value – absolute growth in share price – can be affected by general stock market or sectoral movements;

■ as awards are free, it is possible to deliver value equal to that of share option plans for fewer shares. This can help preserve a company's dilution capacity.

The main disadvantages are:

■ Most use 'market purchase' shares – that is, existing company shares purchased on the market and held by an employees' trust. There will be a cash cost to the company from acquiring the shares to be held in the trust.

■ Many use the market-driven performance measure TSR; executives often regard this as opaque and feel that it does not reflect their performance as directly as EPS growth. As a result, companies are increasingly using alternatives (EPS, profit before tax or PBT, revenue growth, cash flow) to supplement (or sometimes replace) TSR as a performance measure for PSPs. This allows them to retain the advantage of PSP structures while using performance measures that are more 'sympathetic'.

New Share Plans

The table below shows the number of new share plans introduced by FTSE All-Share companies between 2006 and 2009.

	Share Options	PSPs	SMPs
2006	13	88	21
2007	26	80	21
2008	20	54	11
2009	27	17	5

Source: ABI IVIS service.

It is worth noting the tail-off in the total number of new plans introduced in 2009. Clearly, many companies felt that a severe recession was not the time to be introducing new benefits for executives. Interestingly, the number of share option plans held up. Many of these plans were put to shareholders in a low-key way, emphasising that companies were renewing existing plans rather than introducing ones that were wholly new.

(iii) Share Matching Plans (SMPs)

SMPs are similar to PSPs in that they can deliver free shares to executives. The accounting treatment of SMPs is similar to that for PSPs. Also, as with PSPs, performance conditions tend to be based either on TSR or on more stretching EPS conditions than have historically applied to share options plans.

'Standard' SMPs work like this:

■ An executive agrees to defer receipt of a proportion of their annual bonus – or (more rarely) is compelled to do so.

■ The deferred bonus is invested in shares on the executive's behalf and held in trust for a period, usually three years.

■ At the end of the period, the executive receives their invested shares plus a matching award of free shares. Often, the match is 'net to gross' (ie an employee invests from post-tax income but matching awards are of shares worth the gross equivalent).

■ The vesting of the matching award is subject to the achievement of performance conditions.

The main advantages of SMPs are that:

■ they act as retention tools during the deferral period: matching awards are generally forfeited on leaving employment;

■ by investing a proportion of their bonus in shares, the executive effectively pays to participate in the plan and becomes a stakeholder in the future success of the company;

■ given the above, they tend to be favoured by institutional investors.

The main disadvantages are:

■ executives can view them as over-complex;

■ the link to the annual bonus can mean awards are low or even non-existent in difficult years – arguably the times when a company most needs to incentivise and retain executive talent;

■ as with PSPs, there is a potential cash cost to the company and the risk that executives will be dissatisfied with the performance measure.

Performance conditions

The choice of performance conditions is of critical importance.

There are two main types – Earnings Per Share (EPS) growth and Total Shareholder Return (TSR). The principal differences between them are outlined below. In addition, there is an important distinction in the ways they are treated under international accounting standards, and this is explained in the box on page 166.

There is an increasing trend, however, for companies to use a wider range of measures for performance conditions. Investors are willing to accept bespoke measures if an appropriate case can be made. Examples of 'non-standard' performance conditions include profits before tax (PBT), return on capital employed, sales growth and free cash-flow targets.

(i) Earnings Per Share (EPS) Growth

EPS targets are usually expressed as absolute growth targets in excess of growth in the retail prices index over the performance period. They are the common measure for share option schemes, where value is contingent on share price rises.

Key advantages of EPS are that:

■ it is a measure that executives can relate to: it can be directly influenced by the performance of the management team;

■ it is widely recognised, used both by companies internally and by external analysts;

■ the level of targets for vesting awards is set by the company, and the initial hurdle is not a median relative to a peer group that the company cannot control.

Key disadvantages include:

■ fair, long-term targets can be difficult to set. Performance targets that are company-specific and take little account of sectoral or market trends may prove too difficult – or too 'soft'. This is a particular challenge in an economic downturn;

■ executives are not rewarded according to how their company's performance compares with that of its peers;

■ some institutional shareholders fear that EPS is open to manipulation and view TSR as a better means of aligning executives' interests with their own.

(ii) Total Shareholder Return (TSR)

TSR, commonly used with PSPs and SMPs, measures share price growth and dividends. Almost invariably, a company's TSR is compared with that of other companies and ranked. Investors oppose any payment for below median ranking. At median, a proportion of an award will vest (for example, 25 per cent). An upper quartile or higher ranking is required for full (100 per cent) vesting. There is proportionate vesting for achieving rankings between the median and the upper threshold.

TSR targets are typically supported by a secondary target that is a 'financial performance underpin', for example an EPS growth target. Investors are in favour of secondary targets that are company specific to complement TSR, which is market driven.

Key advantages of TSR include:

■ It aligns the interests of shareholders and executives by linking rewards to the returns shareholders make on their investments in the company. This is particularly important in a PSP or SMP, where executives can benefit even if the share price remains static or falls.

■ Many investors prefer it.

■ Performance is measured on a relative basis, so setting long-term targets is reasonably straightforward – ie full vesting occurs at upper quartile performance, partial vesting occurs at median performance, etc.

Key disadvantages include:

■ While institutional shareholders insist that awards lapse even if the company's TSR performance is only just below the median of its chosen comparator group, a substantial proportion of an award (for example, 25 per cent) can vest at median performance. A small differentiation in performance can therefore have a huge impact on payments to executives.

■ Finding an appropriate comparator group can be difficult.

■ As the measure is share-price-dependent it is influenced by market sentiment towards particular sectors, which will not necessarily reflect a company's underlying financial performance. Within a peer group, takeovers or mergers can have a disproportionate impact.

Impact of IFRS on Performance Conditions

Under international accounting standard IFRS 2, TSR is treated as a 'market-based' condition and EPS as a 'non-market based' condition. This leads to an important difference in the way the share plans are charged to the profit and loss account.

■ There is an initial discount factor for a TSR performance condition in the formula used to calculate the 'expected value' charge. This level of charge is then fixed and accrued over the vesting period. There is no ability to 'true-up' (ie to adjust accruals) where an award does not actually vest because the performance condition was not met.

■ There is no initial discount for an EPS performance condition. However, in calculating their annual accruals, companies must estimate the extent to which they believe awards will vest, thereby reducing the level of charge. Accruals can be trued-up so that the final level of charge taken is only for awards that vest.

While this is a very important distinction, opinions vary as to whether it means EPS or TSR is the more attractive option.
  For example:

■ certain companies will prefer to use EPS as they wish to have a charge only for awards that vest;

■ others will prefer to use TSR – the fixed nature of the charge means that the effect on profit and loss will be less volatile.

8

Pensions

This chapter is divided into three parts. The first gives some basic factual information on pension schemes and on the pensions tax regime. The second examines the duties of directors who are trustees of a company pension fund. The third looks at the legal position of directors when a company pension pot falls short.

Part One: The Basics

Pensions often go to the bottom of the pile. They are just too complicated, there are too many decisions to make and the jargon is off-putting. But pensions are crucially important: they can be the single biggest expense of a company and one of the most valuable elements of remuneration. You ignore them at your peril.

1. Main types of pension scheme

A defined benefit or final salary scheme promises a set level of pension once you reach retirement age – no matter what happens to the stock market and the value of investments. The benefit is usually calculated as a proportion of your final salary for each year of service. For example, if you are promised 1/60th of final salary for each year you work for the company and you work for 40 years, you will be paid 40/60ths (ie two-thirds) of your final salary. On top of that, the law requires an element of inflation-proofing to be built in.

In effect, as long as you keep your side of the bargain and make the required level of contributions (typically about five or six per cent of pay), the employer takes all the risk.

There's a downside, though. The employer's contributions may not be enough to guarantee the pension promise in all circumstances. If the scheme winds up, the huge cost of paying everyone's pension may well be beyond its means. What's more, members don't own a share of the fund: where a scheme winds up in deficit, monies are divvied up in accordance with a statutory priority order.

The Pension Protection Fund (PPF) offers compensation when employers go out of business, but this is subject to limits: your entitlement from the PPF won't necessarily match your entitlement under the pension scheme.

The funding problems associated with defined benefit/final salary schemes mean they're rapidly going out of fashion. As Part 3, page 182, makes clear, organisations that have them are closing them to new members.

A money purchase or defined contribution scheme makes no promise about what you will get when you retire. You simply contribute to the pension scheme. The money is then invested in the way you have asked. At retirement, you buy a pension with whatever funds are available. The income you get depends on how well the investments have done and how much it costs to buy the pension, as well as other factors such as whether you want any dependant to get a pension on your death and whether you want inflation-proofing built in. So, in money purchase schemes, it's the pension scheme member who takes all the risk. He or she does have a legal right to a share of the funds, but there is no certainty about what it will be.

Money purchase schemes can be run by employers or by insurance companies. Those run by insurance companies are known as personal pension plans or stakeholder schemes. Your employer may contribute; or it may not.

Cash balance schemes combine elements of the two types of scheme above. They are designed along the lines of a money purchase scheme but the employer promises a certain investment return up to retirement. They are quite popular in the United States but have yet to become part of the mainstream in the United Kingdom. In essence, both the member and employer share the risk.

2. Unfunded schemes

An unfunded scheme is, as its name implies, not pre-funded. It's little more than a paper promise. The employer promises to pay a certain pension at retirement, but does not put aside any money to do so. This is all very well if your employer is the government, but risky if you work in the private sector. (Unlike the government, private companies can go bust.) A financial promise is only as good as the organisation behind it.

3. Tax breaks

To encourage contributions to schemes, the government offers tax breaks. Anything you pay into a scheme will receive tax relief at your higher marginal income tax rate (although there are now restrictions on tax relief for high earners – see section 4 below). Investment returns within the scheme are also tax free. Employers get corporation tax relief on what they contribute.

4. Rules and restrictions

To discourage abuse of the system, there are restrictions on the amount of pension that can be built up each year.

Annual allowance

The annual allowance is the amount of pension you will be allowed to build up each year without incurring tax.

For money purchase schemes, this limit applies to the contributions that you or your employer make. Increases in investments within the scheme are ignored.

For defined benefit schemes, the annual allowance is the annual increase in the capital value of your benefit. The capital value is basically how much more your pension is worth. The government has set down in legislation how this will be calculated.

The annual allowance was £245,000 for the tax year 2009–10. It was increased to £255,000 for 2010–11 and the subsequent five years.

Lifetime allowance

There's also a limit on the amount of pension that can be built up during your life. This was £1.75m for 2009–10, rising to £1.8m for the years 2010–11 to 2015–16.

The amount of pension that you build up in a money purchase scheme is simply the value of your pension account. If you have a final salary benefit, the capital value is the annual pension you are entitled to receive multiplied by 20, plus the value of any additional lump sum benefit.

Pension funds are tested against the lifetime limit each time a new benefit is paid, on death and if you transfer to an overseas scheme. If you take your benefits in stages – for example, if you reduce your working hours and therefore only take part of your pension entitlement – some of your lifetime limit will be used up each time.

Restriction on tax relief for high earners

Under new rules, effective from 6 April 2011, those earning over £150,000 (including employer contributions) are no longer able to claim full tax relief on their pension contributions. Tax relief is tapered down for those earning between £150,000 and £180,000, falling from the higher rate level to the basic rate level once your earnings reach £180,000. The restriction on the employee's income tax relief applies to both employer and employee contributions.

To prevent people getting around this by making large contributions before April 2011, the government has introduced a special tax charge. If you've earned more than £150,000 in any of the tax years between 2007–08 and 2010–11 and have made an 'unusual' pattern of contributions after 22 April 2009, you're likely to be caught. This was subsequently extended, on 9 December 2009, to those earning over £130,000. The rules are very complicated. If you think that you may be affected, you should seek advice as soon as possible.

Compliance and tax collection

The onus is on **individuals** to ensure that they are within the limits or pay the necessary tax. Pension schemes are also responsible for the payment of the lifetime charge.

The **annual allowance tax** is calculated through the self-assessment system. Tax will be charged at 40 per cent on any contributions above the annual allowance.

The **lifetime allowance tax** charge is only payable on pension benefits above the lifetime limit. If you decide to take the excess as a lump sum there will be a one-off tax charge of 55 per cent. If you opt for an additional pension, you will incur a tax charge of 25 per cent on the excess capital value. On top of this, you will be liable for income tax on the additional pension.

Protection of benefits accrued before 2006

Most of the current rules date from 6 April 2006, so-called 'A day', when a new pensions regime came into force. The government allowed people who were then already close to or above the lifetime limit – £1.5m for 2006–07 – to protect their 'retrospective' pension investments, although the window for registering for protection closed on 5 April 2009. There are two forms of protection available, **enhanced** and **primary protection**. In order to retain any protection you have registered for, you will need to continue to comply with certain requirements – you should seek independent financial advice if this is relevant to you.

The investment regime

Investment rules for a pension scheme include:

■ a limit on scheme borrowing to 50 per cent of scheme assets at the date of loan;

■ a five per cent restriction on shares of the sponsoring employer.

Schemes are permitted to invest in residential property, subject to trustee approval.

Phased retirement

Since 6 April 2006, you've been able to continue working and draw a pension – in full or in part. In theory, at least, directors can now step down gradually and carry on in a part-time capacity, perhaps as a non-executive.

Such flexibility is only possible if your scheme allows it, and many defined benefit schemes have now changed their rules, particularly in the light of age discrimination legislation. Money purchase and personal pension schemes are also likely to offer this flexibility. You will need to check the terms of your plan.

Minimum retirement age

Under rules effective from April 2010, the earliest age at which most people can draw their pension is 55 (the previous minimum was 50).

You can only get benefits before you reach 55 if:

■ You are eligible for an ill-health or incapacity pension. (The rules for this are fairly prescriptive and will be set out in the pension scheme booklet.)

■ The law gives you a protected right to retire earlier.

The requirements for meeting the second criterion are detailed and depend (among other things) on whether there was an unqualified right to retire under the rules of your pension scheme at 10 December 2003. (If you exercise this right, you will need to take all of your benefits at the same time and leave employment completely.) The lifetime allowance will be reduced by 2.5 per cent for each year you take the pension before the age of 55.

Tax-free cash payment

It's possible to take up to a quarter of your pension fund (including any additional contributions you have paid) as a tax-free cash payment.

Membership of more than one pension scheme

You are able to join more than one registered pension scheme at the same time – in fact, you are able to join as many as you want. Annual tax relief will be given on the higher of £3,600 (the threshold for total yearly contributions to pension schemes) and your UK earnings (subject to the overall annual allowance limit).

Income drawdown

The majority of members of a personal pension plan or a defined contribution scheme buy an annuity with their pension funds on retirement.

An annuity is a product, usually sold by insurance companies, that promises a certain income until death. What you get therefore depends on how expensive annuities are at the time you retire. Whether they are good value depends on how long you live. If you live a long time, you will do very well. Some people, however, do not survive long after retirement and so do not do so well (even if their wife, husband or partner gets a pension after their death). It's all a bit of a gamble.

Not surprisingly, annuities have been unpopular with some retirees. To make things fairer, the government offers an alternative known as income drawdown, which lets you put off buying an annuity and take some of your pension as income each year.

Once you reach 75 you will be able to buy what is known as an alternatively secured pension (ASP), which allows you to continue drawing income from your pension pot but in a reduced amount. This helps to ensure the funds are not used up too quickly. ASPs must be used to provide an income in retirement and not to pass on capital tax free to dependants.

Income drawdown is a tricky area as the rules are complicated. In addition, you need to have sufficient funds to make the costs worthwhile. And your income will fluctuate in line with the performance of your investments.

If you think income drawdown is for you, seek advice before making a final decision.

5. Other forms of pension

Small self-administered schemes (SSASs)

SSASs used to be very attractive to controlling directors. They offered a tax-efficient vehicle that allowed directors to be trustees and members of their occupational pension scheme.

Trustee members had control over how the assets were invested, and the restrictions were few.

The relative attractions of SSASs have diminished since 6 April, 2006, when all pension schemes became subject to one investment regime. These schemes will, however, continue to operate for some time.

Executive pension plans (EPPs)

EPPs, when used, were normally set up for directors and senior executives. They are usually contracted into the state scheme and are defined contribution schemes. Like SSASs, they will become less common in future.

Self-invested personal pension plans (SIPPs)

SIPPs are personal pension plans that allow individuals to select their own investments. You must use an external provider to hold the money for you.

SIPPs offer members more control in managing investments and are therefore attractive to people with a good understanding of personal finance and the capital markets. There are, however, tax penalties for investments in residential property, paintings, antiques, etc.

6. Employer's duty to provide a pension: the National Employment Savings Trust (NEST)

Currently, there is no requirement for employers to make contributions to a pension scheme for their staff, although many choose to do so as part of their benefits package.

Employers' only obligation at the moment is to designate a stakeholder pension plan, a money purchase pension scheme typically run by an insurance company. (There are some exceptions for employers who already make contributions to another pension scheme or who have fewer than five employees.)

Everything changes in 2012, however, with the introduction of the National Employment Savings Trust or NEST (previously known as the personal accounts scheme). Employers will for the first time have a statutory duty to contribute to a pension scheme for any of their employees who are over 22 and who earn above a minimum amount (about £5,000). Both employers and employees will be required to contribute, although this obligation will be phased in over a number of years. Total contributions will be limited to £3,600 per employee each year. Employees will join the scheme automatically but will be able to opt out.

Employers will be able to use an alternative pension scheme so long as it meets certain conditions.

It is expected that, as NEST is phased in, the requirements relating to stakeholder plans will be phased out.

7. Pension rights on dismissal

Your pension rights are likely to be found in a number of documents, including those below.

■ **Your service contract:** this should refer to any pension arrangement to which your employer will make contributions. If the arrangement is a personal pension plan or a stakeholder scheme, it will typically give details of the pension provider and the level of contributions. If your company has an occupational scheme, the service contract will probably refer to the pension scheme booklet, where more detailed information can be found. Usually, the contract will give your employer the right to change the pension scheme, either expressly or by invoking the power of amendment in the pension scheme.

■ **The pension scheme booklet:** the trustees of any occupational pension scheme are required by law to give you certain details about the scheme. These include an outline of how to join, the benefits available, how much you will need to contribute and how to make a complaint.

If you are made **redundant or are asked to leave your company** you may be entitled to compensation. Your rights will depend on the circumstances and what your service agreement says (see Chapter 6). You should always seek legal advice.

In summary, you are entitled to be put back into the position you would have been in had your service agreement been properly complied with. So, if you're above the minimum retirement age you may be retiring on pension.

If you're a member of a personal pension, stakeholder or money purchase scheme you should be entitled to compensation for lost pension contributions during any period of notice. This loss will be reduced to reflect the fact that you'll be receiving the contributions as a single lump sum rather than over a period of time.

If you're a member of a defined benefit scheme the position is more complicated. To calculate your pension loss, you need to look at your pension rights at the date you leave and the pension rights you would have had at the end of your notice period. The difference is the pension loss. An actuary will have to calculate the value of this difference, unless you're offered an additional period of service in the pension scheme to cover the notice period. Several factors will need to be taken into account. They include:

■ any pay rises you might have been entitled to during your notice period;

■ the fact that you are being paid the money before you would have been entitled to it;

■ any new job you may get, as this is likely to offer some form of pension;

■ any contributions that you would have had to make during the notice period.

If you're entitled to a pension when you leave employment, your employer is not allowed to take any pension benefits that you receive during your notice period into account when calculating compensation for the loss of your job. This is the case even if you receive an enhanced pension under the scheme rules on dismissal or redundancy. What's more, if your pension at the end of your notice period is less than it would have been had you been allowed to serve out your notice, you may claim for pension loss without any adjustment for the pension payments you receive in the meantime.

(The short case study following, Clark v BET, helps to explain these rules.)

Case Notes: Clark v BET

John Clark was the chief executive and managing director of the facilities management company BET. He had a three-year notice period.

In 1996, BET was taken over by rival company Rentokil, and the

> 55-year-old Clark was fired without notice – ie wrongfully dismissed. Clark sued BET for damages.
>
> A provision in Clark's defined benefit pension scheme allowed him to take immediate retirement on an unreduced pension if he were made redundant after a takeover. This meant Clark's pension rights at 55 were more valuable than they would have been if he had retired at the end of his notice period. (Usually, pensions are reduced to take account of early payment.)
>
> Clark was entitled to receive the pension unreduced at 55. His compensation award was not lowered to take this increased pension into account. He was also entitled to claim for pension loss. The pension loss alone was worth £550,000.

Part Two: A Trustee's Duties

Directors often have an interest in pensions that goes beyond their interest in their own pension entitlement. Many are trustees of the company pension scheme. This inevitably means additional duties and additional risks. Often, the implications are not fully appreciated when the appointment is offered and accepted.

The risks can be extreme. In one of the leading trust law cases, a set of trustees acted in accordance with advice received from a leading barrister about their duties. An aggrieved beneficiary complained, and the matter ultimately reached the House of Lords, who by a three to two majority agreed with the beneficiary. As a result, the trustees were ordered to repay millions to the trust. One of the trustees committed suicide in the face of bankruptcy.

Although the case was highly unusual – it's rare to hear of trustees being sued in a personal capacity – it illustrates the pressures and responsibilities involved. Some protection is available (see section 9, below) but trusteeship is not a role to take lightly, and you should think carefully before accepting the appointment.

8. The nature of trusteeship

The trustees hold the legal title of the pension scheme assets and have stringent legal duties to ensure that those assets are used to provide benefits in accordance with the terms of the trust (as overridden by statute).

Essentially, a pension scheme trustee's duties are to:

■ hold the trust assets;

■ invest the assets in accordance with the terms of the trust, and prudently;

■ collect the contributions as required by the terms of the trust;

■ pay the benefits in accordance with the terms of the trust.

Trustees are also legally required to be familiar with the pension scheme's documentation and have an understanding of the legal, funding and investment obligations relating to the scheme. They will need to keep records to show the pensions regulator that they have complied.

Essentially, the legal requirements mean that you should read the trust deed and rules of the pension scheme carefully before becoming a trustee. While most trust deeds are not exactly page-turners, this is an effort you really must make (not least because the regulator now requires you to).

If you do not understand anything, ask questions. You would be surprised how often the wording is out of date, ambiguous or just plain wrong. Since statute often overrides the terms of the trust, you should make sure you get trustee training and legal advice where necessary.

Every pension lawyer will advise you to take these steps, and every pension lawyer will concede that most clients take no notice. The late Peter Carter-Ruck, specialist in libel law, was heard frequently to observe that he ran his office off the clients who took his advice and his Rolls-Royce off the clients who did not. The same observation could be made, on this point at least, by pension lawyers.

9. Personal liability

Forms of protection

As noted above, trustees potentially put everything on the line. To what extent can they protect themselves?

There are three different types of protection: indemnities, insurance and exoneration clauses. An indemnity, whether contained in a trust deed or in a side-letter, acknowledges that a third party (the pension scheme or the employer or some other party) will ensure that a trustee is not out of pocket if he or she is found liable in given circumstances.

Trustee insurance is, to all intents and purposes, just another form of indemnity.

The concept of indemnities and insurance will be relatively familiar to directors, exoneration clauses less so. In contrast to an indemnity, where the trustee remains liable but someone else pays, an exoneration means, as its name suggests, that the trustee escapes liability completely.

Trustees benefit from a statutory exoneration, which says that if it appears to the court that a trustee is personally liable for any breach of trust, but has acted honestly and reasonably, and ought fairly to be excused, then the court may relieve them from personal liability. The problem is that this provision does not automatically apply. It's only effective if a particular court, in its discretion, decides to make use of it.

Additionally, trustees may have the benefit of express exoneration provisions in the pension scheme rules. However, the courts will not interpret such clauses as allowing trustees to act in bad faith or recklessly. Trustees who think they can get away with anything because they are protected by the exoneration clause are badly misguided.

An exoneration clause does not prevent the pensions regulator from imposing a fine for breach of one of the particular statutory provisions over which it has control. Fines by the pensions regulator, however, are rare and can only apply where trustees have failed to take 'all such steps as are reasonable to secure compliance' with the particular statutory duty.

Exoneration provisions do not apply to trustees' investment functions. But if trustees delegate decisions about investments to a fund manager, they will not be responsible for any defaults by that fund manager if they have taken all reasonable steps to ensure that he or she:

■ has the appropriate knowledge and experience for managing the scheme investments;

■ carries out his or her work competently; and

■ has regard to the need for proper diversification of investments.

Limits to protection

Indemnities and exoneration clauses can have substantially different effects. An indemnity (or insurance) is only as good as the person who undertakes to pay out. Where the indemnifier does not have the funds to provide the necessary cover, it's useless. Where the indemnifier is unwilling to pay out, the trustees may find themselves in serious difficulties and may need to take legal action to recover the money.

An exoneration clause, on the other hand, requires no action by the trustees. Claims against trustees by a beneficiary will be unable to succeed since they will not be liable for their mistakes. Exoneration provisions, however, won't cover you for all acts or in all circumstances. Further, they only protect you against claims by members or the employer: they will not help if, for example, your investment managers make a complaint.

From the viewpoint of pension scheme members, indemnities are often seen as more desirable than exoneration clauses: exoneration clauses can leave schemes seriously out of pocket for the mistakes of trustees.

Trustee indemnity insurance can potentially give added protection to the trustees if they cannot rely on their indemnity protection. The insurer may reimburse the trustees for any successful claim brought against them by a beneficiary.

Trustees should bear in mind, though, that insurance cover is normally heavily skewed in favour of the insurer. Insurers have almost never made a payment to trustees under an indemnity insurance policy. The golden rule is: prevention is better than cure. Administer the scheme properly and make sure you're happy with the exoneration provisions, and claims won't be upheld against you in the first place.

10. Corporate trustees

There is no rule of law that says that trustees need to be individuals. It's entirely possible to have a company as a trustee, and many pension schemes operate in this way, with the individuals who would have been trustees acting as directors of the trustee company. This has significant advantages for the trustee directors, though it has some drawbacks, too.

The main advantage is that it's the company that's liable to scheme members, not the trustee directors. The trustee directors' only duties are to the trustee company. The duties of a director are a little less exacting than the duties of a trustee (although, as this book shows, they're still pretty onerous).

The main disadvantage is that company law is much more restrictive than trust law about the extent to which people can be indemnified or exonerated by companies of which they're directors (see section 13 of Chapter 2). There are also additional requirements under company law relating to conflicts of interests (see section 4 of Chapter 2). These must be complied with in addition to the general conflict requirements applying to all trustees (see below).

11. Conflicts of interest

Trustees should exercise their powers in order to further the purposes of the pension scheme. The courts have developed strict tests to ensure they do this.

One of the duties of trustees is not to put themselves in a position where there is a conflict between their duties and their private interests. The court will not consider whether or not the trustee has allowed their external interest to influence the decision making – the fact that they have acted while in a position of conflict of interest will be enough to constitute a breach of trust.

For directors, this can be a particularly difficult problem. If a director is a trustee and a member of the pension scheme, on any given issue they may have multiple competing interests (for example, the setting of employer contribution rates at a time when company finances are hard-pressed).

The problem has been addressed in part by statute, and the courts have also set out a limited exception to the strict conflict of interest rule. Neither of these changes offers a complete solution to the problems faced by directors: extreme care still needs to be taken.

Trustees who are also members of their pension scheme (as the majority of them are) frequently have theoretical conflicts between their personal interests as members and their duties as trustees. The government has therefore given statutory protection to such trustees.

But this is less helpful than it may appear. It applies only to a member's interest as a member. A trustee who owes director's duties to the employer would not be protected. Also, trustees must still exercise their powers in order to further the purposes of the pension scheme. Those who act in their own interests and against the interests of the scheme will find themselves in deep trouble.

Separately, the courts have also been looking to the commercial realities of pension scheme trusteeship and showing a markedly more sympathetic approach. Where pension scheme rules state that the trustees must include people who hold the role of director (or equivalent) and the conflict of interest is slight, there may be some leniency. (See the brief case study, Edge v Pensions Ombudsman, opposite.)

Of course, there are occasions where your interests and duties conflict starkly. Just how should you approach the setting of employer contribution rates at a time when company finances are hard-pressed? The company's and the pension scheme's interests may be diametrically opposed. As a director/trustee, you owe duties to both. If you find yourself in such a conflict, you should take legal advice as to whether you need to step aside from the decision-making process, or even resign one of your posts.

Between the cases where the conflict is slight (for example, deciding whether to grant a small increase to all members' benefits, including your own) and the cases where the conflict is extreme, are many intermediate cases. How should you decide whether you can safely act or not?

There is a simple rule of thumb: if you find yourself badly wanting to be involved in the decision, you should probably stand aside.

Case Notes: Edge v Pensions Ombudsman, 1999

The Court of Appeal considered the problem of trustees' conflicts of interest in Edge v Pensions Ombudsman, where the pension scheme rules required the trustees to hold or have held an office equivalent to that of director.

The court recognised that decisions of such trustees would inevitably be perceived by some to favour one interest at the expense of another. It concluded that the only sensible answer was to accept that the scheme was established on the basis that the pension rules were intended to provide a body of trustees that could be relied upon to consider all interests fairly and properly; and that those who seek to challenge a decision of that body should bear the ordinary burden of establishing that the decision has been reached improperly.

If your pension scheme rules specify the composition of the trustee body, this ruling could come to your assistance in cases where the conflict between the different duties isn't serious.

---

12. Confidentiality of information

Related to the problem of conflicts of interest is that of confidential information.

Trustees are obliged to use all the information at their disposal when considering trustee business and making decisions, and to share anything of relevance with their fellow trustees.

But what if you know something that's both relevant and confidential? The simplest solution is to persuade the company to allow you to release information to fellow trustees 'for their eyes only'. If this isn't possible, you should seek legal advice – and do so promptly.

13. Giving advice to employees

There are specific statutory obligations relating to the disclosure of information, which your pensions advisers can help you with. And the pensions regulator and the Financial Services Authority (FSA) are encouraging employers to promote their pension schemes to their staff. But perhaps surprisingly, neither trustees nor employers are under any general legal duty to advise pension scheme members about their pension rights.

In fact, it's good practice not to advise members about their rights at all. It's all too easy to fall into the trap of handing out advice of the type that's regulated by the FSA and which most directors and trustees are not authorised to give. Still more dangerously, you could run the risk of giving the wrong advice because you do not know all of the facts. An employee may keep crucial bits of information about their personal circumstances hidden from you – for example, the fact that they are about to hand in their notice.

Sometimes, the advice could run directly counter to the interests of other members. Trustees should not favour one group at the expense of another.

The best policy, despite the natural human instinct to be helpful, is therefore to avoid giving advice to pension scheme members, no matter how much they look for a steer from you. And do not make the mistake of giving advice 'off the record' – you are just as liable for what you say off the record as you are for what you say on it.

Part Three: Liabilities for Underfunding

The combined effects of rising life expectancy and falling investment values have meant the costs of running a defined benefit scheme have grown significantly in recent years. Many companies feel they simply can't sustain these costs in the future. As a result, schemes are being shut and staff are being put into cheaper alternatives.

Once the scheme has been shut, the employer will continue to be responsible for its costs until it's wound up. Winding up the scheme may look like an attractive option, but often it isn't viable for the employer. An employer that winds up its scheme (whether or not this is part of its long-term benefits strategy) has a legal duty to top up the pension scheme funding so that the trustees can fully secure all members' benefits with annuities bought from insurance companies. (At the time of writing, the cost of securing benefits in this way is far greater than the cost of providing them from an ongoing pension scheme.) The amount of the top-up required from the employer is known as the statutory debt.

The level of this statutory debt can be very high – high enough, indeed, to bankrupt the business.

Pension schemes that cover more than one employer in the corporate group can also run into problems. Where a group company has very few employees left in the pension scheme and the last one leaves or dies, the employer will immediately become liable for its share of the statutory debt. An employer in this situation does have a 12-month period to allow another of its employees to join the scheme, but if it intends to take advantage of this option it must let the trustees know within one month. There is no leeway over either of these time periods.

Frequently, the initial one-month deadline is missed because an employer has not noticed that their last employee has left the scheme. It may not be clear from scheme records who was actually employing the particular individual (especially if records are poor or if the person worked for more than one employer). It is therefore important that employers who may find themselves in this position ensure that there is a system to inform them immediately when the last person leaves.

The pensions regulator has sweeping powers to bring into line companies that try to arrange their affairs to avoid the statutory debt. In theory, at least, no attempt to evade pension liabilities will go unnoticed. (See section 14, below.)

Directors should take underfunding very seriously. It's not something that will go away by itself and could well take up a significant amount of management time. It could also cost the company a lot of money and, in some circumstances, even its 'life'.

14. The regulator's powers

- **Contribution notices:** these can be served on other group companies and individuals where action has been taken that avoids the payment of a statutory debt or makes it less likely that members will be able to receive their full entitlements. As will be clear from the above, a statutory debt is triggered when an employer leaves the pension scheme – for example, when there is a takeover or company sale – and the value of the scheme's assets won't secure all members' benefits with an insurance company. The debt will be far higher than any deficit disclosed in the company's accounts under FRS17 or IAS19.

- **Financial support directions:** if the regulator considers that the pension scheme employer is either a service company or insufficiently resourced to pay any debt that may arise, it can issue a financial support direction against other companies in the group.

- **Restoration orders:** where money or property has been transferred from a pension scheme at an undervalue in the two years before an insolvency event or application for protection from the Pension Protection Fund, the regulator can order its return.

Anyone who may be subject to either a contribution notice or a financial support direction will be able to seek a clearance statement from the regulator. This, however, will not guarantee immunity. (See section 16, below.)

15. The position of individual directors

The regulator does not have the power to make a financial support direction against an individual unless the employer is a sole trader or a partnership.

It does, though, have wide powers to impose contribution notices against individuals. To be caught, you need to be 'connected' or 'associated' with an employer in the pension scheme. Connected or associated in this context is very widely defined. Any director or employee could qualify, but shareholders are exempt unless they 'control' the company – ie own at least one-third of the voting shares.

Shareholders can also be caught if they and someone associated or connected with them (for example, a spouse) own one-third of the shares together.

16. Reducing the risk of liability

There are several things individuals and companies can do to reduce the likelihood of action by the regulator.

Request a clearance statement from the regulator

The regulator expects clearance to be sought only when a particular action is materially detrimental to the ability of a defined benefit pension scheme to meet its liabilities. The triggering event must fall within certain categories that are described by the pensions regulator in its published guidance. In some cases, the pension scheme itself must be in deficit. Any clearance will apply until there is a 'material change in circumstances'. The consequences of this remain unclear; it could, though, reduce the usefulness of the clearance statement.

Take advice

The regulator can only make a contribution notice against an individual if it is reasonable to do so. It will need to look at your financial circumstances, the purpose of the act complained of (for example, to limit the loss of employment) and your involvement in the scheme or its failure. If you are contemplating doing anything that may mean pension scheme liabilities are avoided, you should seek legal advice first.

Companies should also take their own advice as soon as possible. Trustees of the pension scheme will probably have already consulted their actuarial (and possibly legal) advisers and may try to demand more money from the company. The company may be able to negotiate with the trustees, but this will depend on its financial position, the extent of the underfunding and the terms of the pension scheme itself.

Professional advisers such as actuaries, lawyers and benefit consultants will be familiar with the issues involved and will be able to suggest ways of managing the underfunding to fit the company's circumstances.

Given that the exercise can take up a lot of management time, it may be worth putting together a small, dedicated team to look at the issue and keep the rest of the board informed. Such a team would obviously need to include the finance director.

Talk to the trustees

The trustees will be concerned to put any underfunding in the pension scheme right. They have duties to the members; and they have statutory duties to report underfunding or non-payment of contributions to the pensions regulator. Equally, they will not want to push the company into insolvency as that would mean job losses (and would also make it more difficult to get any money out of the company). Trustees have become more aware of this balancing act, and the pensions regulator has published guidance to help them and the employer.

The amount that the trustees can ask for will be governed both by legislation and by the documentation of the pension scheme itself. Legislation requires defined benefit schemes to be funded in accordance with the 'statutory funding objective'. This is a scheme-specific system, which the trustees must agree with the employer. The process for setting it is fairly prescriptive, and the pensions regulator has issued detailed guidance about what it expects.

The trustees have a lot of power in the process of making sure funding requirements are met. However, they will sometimes agree to a lower payment by the employer if it will keep the scheme open and the company in business. The pensions regulator will need to be involved in any such agreement. Again, seeking advice early is invaluable.

Comply with the regulator's reporting requirements

Trustees, employers and other professional advisers involved in the pension scheme must notify the pensions regulator of certain matters. Failure to do so could leave the offender liable to a civil fine. Issues that need to be notified by employers are wide-ranging and include any decision to compromise a scheme debt, any breach of the employer's banking covenant and a change of control of a pension scheme employer.

9

Health and Safety and Corporate Manslaughter

Health and safety is a highly regulated area and should be a priority for the board. Putting employees, customers and others at risk by not following the rules can amount to a criminal offence, with the potential for substantial (possibly multi-million pound) fines for the company, and fines and/or imprisonment for individual directors and employees.

The approach to health and safety must be rigorous. It's important that both internal and external risks are identified and actively managed. This will mean working with contractors and suppliers to eliminate bad practice: weak links in the supply chain leave you vulnerable and increase your risk of prosecution.

Significant changes to the framework of health and safety legislation have been made in the past few years, increasing further the challenges faced by companies and their directors.

The following sections look at what the law expects; and at the consequences when it's breached.

1. A company's duties

Every company has a general duty to ensure the health, safety and welfare of its employees, customers, contractors and anyone else who may be affected by its activities. But there's an important qualification to this duty: it applies only 'so far as is reasonably practicable'. The law is interested only in material risks to health and safety that any reasonable person would appreciate and take steps to guard against. Fanciful or hypothetical risks can be ignored (see case notes, R v Chargot Limited, opposite).

This limitation on the general duty to guard against material risk – 'so far as is reasonably practicable' – allows a business to weigh a particular risk against the cost of preventative action in terms of time, money and effort. If that cost would be grossly disproportionate to the reduction in risk achieved, a decision not to take the action will be justified, and there will be no breach of the general duty.

It's important to emphasise that, although prosecutions are frequently brought as a result of an accident in which someone has been hurt, a company can be liable where no personal injury has occurred. All the prosecution need prove is that a **state of affairs** existed that posed a real risk to the health or safety of employees or others. It is the risk of harm that is key, not that actual harm has been caused.

As well as this general duty to ensure the health, safety and welfare of employees and others, there are other more specific duties that will apply to many businesses, depending on the particular hazards and risks associated with each – the box on pages 189 and 190 lists some of the areas covered.

These more detailed regulations often impose absolute obligations to put a specific safety measure in place or to avoid a particular hazard. In contrast with the general duty described above, doing everything reasonably practical to comply may not be sufficient.

In addition, every employer is required to implement a management system for identifying and managing risks. In practice, that means ensuring that:

- risk assessments are made;

- employers have access to competent health and safety advice;

- employees are provided with relevant information and training;

- risks specific to certain employees – for example, new and expectant mothers or the young – are assessed separately.

Case Notes: R v Chargot Limited

Shaun Riley was driving a dumper truck at a farm near Chorley in Lancashire, shifting soil to create a car park. After a few successful trips, the truck tipped over and he was killed by the load he was carrying. There were no witnesses to what happened. He had not been trained, he was unsupervised and he was not wearing the seat belt that would almost certainly have saved him.

Three parties were prosecuted for health and safety offences: his employer, the site contractor and the contractor's managing director. The prosecution rested its case on the fact of the accident – the employee's death was enough to show that there had been a breach of the duty to ensure his health and safety. The burden of proof then passed to the defendants to establish, on the balance of probabilities, that it was not reasonably practicable for them to do more than they did to prevent the tragedy.

The court supported this view, holding that, to be successful, the prosecution had to do no more than identify a risk to the health and safety of employees or the public, provided it was a material risk that any reasonable person would appreciate and take steps to guard against. Further details as to the precise acts and omissions that caused the death were unnecessary. Proof of accident or injury will generally be enough to show the risk was material, not hypothetical. The burden is then on the business to show that it took all reasonably practical steps to prevent it.

The employer was fined £75,000 and ordered to pay costs of £37,500; the contractor paid a fine of £100,000 and costs of £75,000; the managing director's fine was set at £75,000 with costs of £103,000.

Risk-specific Duties

In addition to the general duty described earlier, more specific health and safety duties will apply to many businesses. A selection follows, with web addresses for the relevant guidance notes.

Fire safety – if you are an employer and own, control or manage premises, you must take reasonable steps to reduce the risk of fire and ensure there is a safe escape route if fire occurs. Fire risk assessments must be carried out. This applies to all buildings, structures and open spaces, but not to individual private dwellings.

www.opsi.gov.uk/si/si2005/20051541.htm

Injuries, diseases and dangerous occurrences – employers, the self-employed and those in control of premises must record and report to the Health and Safety Executive all deaths, major injuries, 'over three-day injuries' (those that result in someone not being able to undertake their normal work for more than three consecutive days), diseases and near-miss accidents (known as 'dangerous occurrences') that relate to work activities. www.hse.gov.uk/pubns/priced/l73.pdf

Work equipment – if you provide equipment at work, you have a duty to prevent or control risks arising from its use. You need to ensure that it's suitable for its intended purpose and that it's inspected and safely maintained. What's more, you must provide adequate information and training for those who use it. www.opsi.gov.uk/si/si1998/19982306.htm

Display screen equipment and work stations – employers must carry out a risk assessment for work stations and provide adequate health and safety training for those using them. They must also ensure users take regular screen breaks and are informed of their entitlement to annual eye tests paid for by the company.
www.opsi.gov.uk/si/si1992/Uksi_19922792_en_1.htm

Manual handling – employees must be given adequate training on safe handling and lifting techniques and told to follow the company's health and safety systems and policies. www.opsi.gov.uk/SI/si1992/Uksi_19922793_en_1.htm

2. A director's personal liability

The liability described in the preceding section is a liability of the business, usually a corporate body in one form or another. But where a company is shown to have committed a health and safety offence, an individual director may also be found to have committed a criminal offence (and this applies equally to a company secretary, manager or anyone else acting in a similar capacity).

The case against a director can be proved if the offence by the company was:

■ **committed with their consent** – they were aware of the circumstances and positively endorsed it;

■ **committed with their connivance** – they were aware of the circumstances but turned a blind eye;

■ **attributable to their neglect** – they should have been aware of the circumstances and taken action.

Despite this personal liability when things go wrong, the positive obligation to manage a business in a way that ensures the health and safety of employees and others still rests with the company, not its directors. There is no guarantee this will continue, though: the health and safety duties of individual directors are constantly under review.

3. Penalties

A breach of health and safety law is a criminal offence, punishable in the case of a business by a fine. In recent years, fines have increased, and the courts have made clear that they should be large enough both to reflect the culpability of the business and to get the attention of the shareholders.

Where the offence involves a fatality, fines between £100,000 and £500,000 are increasingly common; larger companies can expect to pay more than £1m (see the box on the Hatfield rail crash and Balfour Beatty, page 192, and section 6, page 197, on guidance from the Sentencing Guidelines Council).

Prosecutions for health and safety offences may be dealt with in the Magistrates' Court or the Crown Court. In the former, the maximum fine is now £20,000 for most offences, which may in itself lead to a greater number of prosecutions. A broader range of cases can now be taken to the Crown Court, exposing defendants to higher, unlimited fines.

A business found to have breached health and safety law can also be issued with an enforcement notice that either requires:

■ specific action to be taken in a set time period; or

■ a specific activity to stop or the use of particular plant or equipment to cease.

A director found guilty of consent, connivance or neglect is liable for an unlimited fine and to a prison sentence of up to two years. Fines won't be covered by a directors' and officers' insurance policy, or by any indemnity from the company (see Chapter 2, section 13), and, of course, no-one can serve a prison sentence for you. To make matters worse, once found guilty you can be disqualified from acting as a director for up to 15 years.

So the consequences of a health and safety lapse by a director can be severe: a hefty fine, prison, and a long-term obstacle to earning a living.

Case Notes: The Hatfield Rail Crash and Balfour Beatty

Four people were killed when cracked rail tracks caused a train to derail approaching Hatfield station. Balfour Beatty was responsible for maintaining the tracks. A faulty rail had been identified 21 months before the crash and a replacement rail had been delivered to the site six months before, but the repair had never been carried out.

Balfour Beatty was prosecuted for health and safety breaches, and the judge described its performance as 'one of the worst examples of sustained industrial negligence in a high-risk industry [he had] ever seen'. The company pleaded guilty and was fined £10m; Network Rail protested its innocence but was convicted by a jury and fined £3.5m. Balfour Beatty appealed and had its fine reduced to £7.5m.

The Court of Appeal judgment was not that a £10m fine for a systemic failure was wrong in principle but that it bore too little relationship to the Network Rail penalty. (The implication was that the Court thought the latter was too low, but fairness dictated that it reduce the former to bring the two more into line.)

Among other points to come out of the ruling is that fines should be large enough to raise concerns among shareholders – but that need not necessarily mean that they must be so large as to reduce the next dividend or hit the share price.

---

4. Corporate manslaughter

At its worst, a breach of the health and safety rules has tragic consequences, leading to the loss of life. Historically, though, it's been hard to convict a company of corporate manslaughter (or corporate homicide in Scotland); the *Herald of Free Enterprise* disaster, the King's Cross fire and various rail crashes have all highlighted the problems.

The prosecution had to prove two things: first, that a single individual in the company was guilty of gross negligence manslaughter; second, that this individual was the 'controlling mind' of the company. If there was not enough evidence to convict an individual, there could be no prosecution of the company.

Larger companies therefore frequently escaped conviction as fatal accidents are often the result of failures by a number of people over a period of time. The larger the company, the greater the number; and the less likely the chance of proving that a single person, representing the company's controlling mind, had been grossly negligent.

After much delay, the law in this area was reformed by the **Corporate Manslaughter and Corporate Homicide Act 2007**, which came into force on 6 April 2008. A year later, the first prosecution of a company was brought under the new law.

Under the 2007 Act, the focus shifts from an individual failing to a broader failure of management, determined by a threefold test. An offence is committed if the way an organisation manages or organises its activities:

■ caused a person's death;

■ amounted to a gross breach of a relevant duty of care owed by the organisation to the victim; and

■ senior management played a substantial part in the breach.

The old law only ever caught small, one-man companies; the new law makes it much more likely that larger organisations with more wide-spread systems of management will be answerable if a failure in their management or organisation causes a death. (Network Rail and Balfour Beatty, for example, would certainly have been at greater risk if they had been prosecuted for corporate manslaughter today – see the box on page 192.) But the requirement for a gross breach of duty provides a safe-guard: if a company has robust systems for managing risks to health and safety and complies with the legislation described in section 1, a pros-ecution for corporate manslaughter remains unlikely.

If convicted, the organisation will be liable to an unlimited fine (see section 6, page 197). In addition, there may be either or both of:

■ a remedial order requiring the organisation to take steps, within a specified time, to remedy the breach and any matter resulting from it that was a cause of death and, possibly, to change policies, systems or practices;

■ a publicity order requiring the organisation to publicise, in a speci-fied manner, the fact it has been convicted of corporate manslaughter together with particulars of the offence, the amount of any fine and the terms of any remedial order made.

The latter is 'naming and shaming' at its most potent.

Leadership and proper engagement by directors and senior manage-ment in both managing health and safety risks and ensuring compliance with health and safety laws will be key in preventing or defending an allegation of corporate manslaughter.

See the following box for further points on the corporate manslaughter offence.

Corporate Manslaughter and Corporate Homicide Act 2007

The Act applies not only to companies, but also to other organisations, including partnerships (where they are employers), local government authorities, NHS Trusts and certain central government departments.

The injury or harm that caused the death must have happened in the United Kingdom. So foreign companies operating in the United Kingdom are caught where the harm occurs here, but the Act does not extend to UK companies operating abroad.

The organisation must have owed a relevant duty of care to the victim. Such a duty will always exist between an employer and its employees, and between a business and its customers or anyone else who uses its goods and services. There is also a duty of care between an occupier of premises and lawful or unlawful visitors to those premises. Indeed, a business will have a duty of care to anyone who is affected by its commercial activities, such as the carrying on of any construction or maintenance work or the use of plant or vehicles.

Senior management are those who play a significant role in deciding how the whole (or a substantial part) of an organisation's activities are managed or organised; also caught are those who actually manage or organise those activities. It is the collective actions and inactions of these board members and managers that will be subject to scrutiny, not the failings of relatively junior staff on the ground.

The management failure has to be bad enough to amount to a gross breach of duty. That means the conduct has to fall far below what could reasonably be expected in the circumstances. In deciding this, a number of factors will be looked at:

■ Was there a failure to comply with relevant health and safety legislation?

■ How serious was the non-compliance?

■ How great was the risk of death caused by the breach?

■ What was the organisation's safety culture – to what extent did attitudes, policies, systems or accepted practices encourage or tolerate the breach?

■ What industry guidance was there, or codes of practice or similar publications issued by bodies such as the Health and Safety Executive, and were they followed?

The gross breach does not have to have been the sole cause of the death but it must have made more than a minimal contribution to it; and senior management must have played a substantial part in that breach.

A prosecution can only be brought with the consent of the Director of Public Prosecutions, so private prosecutions will not be possible.

The offence applies only to organisations. There is no separate offence under the Act for individuals, such as the senior managers whose failures result in the prosecution (though they can still face liability for general health and safety offences, as described in section 2, page 190). This has been a controversial point, with some arguing that the necessary change in culture will only come about when directors face a real threat of jail. One trade union leader has been quoted as saying: 'Directors in the dock is what we want.'

5. Guidance for directors

To help directors deal with health and safety risks, and so avoid liability for themselves and their companies, in 2007 the Health and Safety Executive, the body that enforces health and safety law, teamed up with the Institute of Directors to produce guidelines. *Leading Health and Safety at Work – Leadership Actions for Directors and Board Members* (available online at www.hse.gov.uk/pubns/indg417.pdf) sets out an agenda for effective leadership by the board.

The first step is to set the right 'tone at the top' and for the board to provide effective leadership from the top down. The guidance sets out three 'essential principles' that underpin good health and safety performance:

■ strong and active leadership;

■ worker involvement and engagement;

■ assessment and review.

A four-point agenda can be used to embed these principles into an organisation's culture by:

■ planning the direction for health and safety policy;

■ delivering on health and safety;

■ monitoring performance;

■ reviewing and checking compliance.

As mentioned in the box on pages 194 and 195, directors and senior managers who read this guidance and follow it will give their companies a better chance should they ever be investigated for a gross breach of the duty of care under the corporate manslaughter legislation.

In addition, examples of conduct by directors and senior managers that can avoid or minimise the risk of prosecution include:

■ receiving reports on safety performance and ensuring safety is discussed regularly at board level;

■ leading by example and being visible;

■ seeking and acting on competent advice when making policy and purchasing decisions;

■ thoroughly considering requests for resources and justifying carefully any refusals;

■ providing training to directors and senior managers on their health and safety responsibilities;

■ checking the safety arrangements of key suppliers and contractors;

■ setting personal objectives around safety performance;

■ participating in a clearly defined management system for health and safety.

By contrast, the following are common examples of conduct by directors and senior managers that can lead to their personal prosecution for health and safety offences, or at least to prosecution of their company:

■ allowing safety risks to persist to save money;

■ sanctioning or promoting unsafe working practices;

■ approving and signing off inadequate risk assessments or method statements;

■ failing to take a diligent approach to collective and individual responsibilities.

6. Sentencing guidelines: level of fines

For many years, there has been public disquiet at the level of fines imposed on organisations whose health and safety breaches have caused deaths.

In 2007, the Sentencing Advisory Panel issued a consultation paper on sentencing guidelines for convictions under the then new Corporate Manslaughter Act. A key proposal was for fines to be based on a percentage of the offender's turnover. If adopted, that could have led to multi-million pound penalties for larger organisations. (If the maximum fine of 10 per cent of annual turnover had been applied in the Hatfield train crash case – see the box on page 192 – Network Rail's fine of £3.5m would have risen to £600m and Balfour Beatty's £7.5m fine would have increased to £200m.)

In October 2009, the prospect of turnover-based fines receded when the Sentencing Guidelines Council chose not to follow the Panel's proposals, which they saw as having potentially unfair consequences and being difficult to apply to public-sector and not-for-profit bodies. Instead, they published guidelines of their own in February 2010:

- courts should still look at turnover and profit to get a sense of the company's resources;

- fines should be punitive and big enough to have an effect – but as a general rule they should not be so large as to put companies out of business or cause job losses;

- fines for corporate manslaughter offences 'should seldom be less than £500,000' and may run to millions;

- fines for health and safety offences causing death 'should seldom be less than £100,000' and may run to hundreds of thousands or more;

- fines should be discounted if there is a guilty plea;

- companies should put financial information before the court, particularly figures for turnover, pre-tax profit and director remuneration;

- publicity orders (requiring the organisation to publicise its conviction in the media) should be the norm.

With these guidelines to hand, the court will then:

- judge how serious the breach is;

- apply aggravating and mitigating factors (see below);

- look at the size and resources of the organisation;

- consider the consequences the fine might have;

- arrive at a preliminary figure on that basis;

- make a deduction in the case of a guilty plea;

- consider a publicity order (and a remedial order requiring the organisation to remedy any ongoing failings).

Further information can be found at www.sentencing-guidelines.gov.uk.
 Whether it's a corporate manslaughter or health and safety offence, aggravating factors that will increase the fine include:

- more than one person killed as a result of the offence;

- serious injury to others in addition to the fatality;

- failure to act on previous advice, cautions or warnings from enforcing authorities;

- failure to heed relevant concerns of employees or others;

- action or inaction prompted by financial gain;

- a corporate culture that tolerates a breach of duty.

Mitigating factors that will reduce the organisation's fine include:

- an employee acting outside their authority or failing in their personal duties;

- ready cooperation with the authorities;

- previous good safety record;

- a prompt admission of responsibility followed by a timely guilty plea;

- steps taken after the event to remedy deficiencies once they have been pointed out.

10

Financial Difficulty and Insolvency

This chapter looks at the legal position of directors when a company is in financial trouble or insolvent and explains the main insolvency procedures.

Those who flout the rules and fail in their duty to creditors and shareholders can be ordered to contribute to the company's assets and, in the worst cases, be prosecuted for fraudulent trading.

Sections 1 to 4 below provide a guide to the kind of action (or inaction) that increases the risks of personal liability, but they are not an exhaustive study of the law. Advice will need to be sought in all circumstances.

1. Legal duties

The general duties of directors are examined in detail in Chapter 2. Below, we highlight those most specific to insolvency-related cases.

■ **To consider the interests of creditors above those of members.** When a company is clearly solvent, directors must act in the interests of the shareholders in general. When a company is insolvent and even when it's of doubtful solvency, the position changes: creditors come first.

■ **Not to act for any personal or additional purpose.** All directors should separate their own personal interest (as shareholder, executive, creditor, etc) from the company's interests. Their duty is to act in the interests of the company. This will mean following the principles outlined in section 2 below.

■ **To take steps to avoid loss to creditors.** Under insolvency legislation, a director will be personally liable for wrongful trading if a liquidator can show that they knew or ought to have concluded there was no reasonable prospect of avoiding liquidation but continued to do business as 'normal'. Liability will not arise if the director can show (to the court's satisfaction) that they took every possible step to minimise the potential loss to the company's creditors. They must be seen to have actively tried to do this.

A director should never allow a company to accept credit if in their view there is no reasonable expectation of the creditor being paid at, or shortly after, the time when the debt becomes due. Anyone knowingly party to a transaction in such circumstances could be ordered by the court to make contributions to a company's assets, and be guilty of the criminal offence of fraudulent trading.

■ **Not to enter into transactions at an undervalue or make preferences.** Insolvency legislation permits an administrator or liquidator of a company to apply to a court to set aside or vary transactions at an undervalue as well as preferences entered into within a specified period before insolvency proceedings began. (Transactions at an undervalue and preferences are defined in section 4, page 211.) In setting a transaction aside, a court will make an order to restore the position to what it would have been had the transaction not taken place. This may result in personal liability for the directors of the company and disqualification proceedings against any director responsible for the transaction concerned.

2. Actions that minimise the risks of liability

It's important not only that the steps explained below are carried out, but also that they are seen to be carried out: the behaviour of directors may be carefully scrutinised by a future liquidator or administrator. Actions taken in the interests of a company and its creditors should be methodically documented and explained. All meetings must be minuted. Directors must give reasons for their decisions and cite the advice they have taken. Directors who can show that they acted in good faith on the advice of suitably qualified professionals will be more likely to avoid wrongful trading allegations – even if the liquidator believes the advice they were given was wrong.

Monitoring the financial position of the company

A director should regularly review the company's financial position in order to assess whether the company is solvent and to determine its prospects of avoiding insolvent liquidation. This will generally involve the preparation of regular statements of affairs and cash-flow projections and other current financial information – in collaboration with auditors and other advisers as necessary.

Directors should establish a procedure for the finance director to keep the board informed of the performance and prospects of the company. This will generally involve frequent board meetings.

The directors should be satisfied that, taking into account their duties to creditors, shareholders and employees, the company may properly continue to trade. Each director should carefully consider the company's ability to pay before arranging for the receipt of any further goods or services on credit, and the board should regularly review the company's financial position. These reviews should be fully minuted.

Individual directors should raise any concerns over solvency with the board as a whole. If their fears are not heeded, they should repeat them and take steps to protect their own position (see the paragraph on resignation in the box on page 207).

If directors believe the minutes of a board meeting do not properly reflect the views they put forward, they should ask for correction, and failing that, write to the chairman (copying the letter to other board members) re-stating their position. It's important for there to be a written record of what a dissenting director said, and when, whether it appears in the official board minutes or elsewhere.

When going through a difficult period, directors must regularly ask whether their company fails the 'solvency test'. A company will be regarded as insolvent when it is unable to pay its debts or the value of its assets is less than the amount of its liabilities, taking into account its contingent and prospective liabilities.

A company is deemed to be unable to pay its debts if:

■ a creditor owed more than £750 has served a statutory demand at the company's registered office and the debt has not been paid for three weeks thereafter;

■ execution of a judgment or other court order remains unsatisfied after a visit from a bailiff or sheriff's officer.

If a company is part of a group, it's important for the directors to think of it as a separate legal entity, even where the treasury function is shared. The financial position of each company in the group has to be evaluated separately. This may require a review of facility letters, security, guarantees, joint venture documentation, joint obligations and similar documentation in order to determine the nature and extent of the financial position of each subsidiary.

Taking advice

Directors of a company in financial difficulties often face a dilemma. It seems that they are expected to be neither unduly rash nor unduly cowardly.

Causing a company to cease to trade or putting it into administration or liquidation, or calling in an administrative receiver (discussed on page 216) prematurely can be as damaging to the interests of the creditors as allowing a company to carry on trading against all odds.

Directors must act responsibly, resisting, on the one hand, their natural tendency to be over-optimistic or to refuse to accept defeat and, on the other hand, the temptation to succumb to despair without considering the options available. Their analysis of the company's performance and prospects should be based on up-to-date financial information and should almost certainly involve consultation with professional legal and financial advisers. Advisers can offer a range of 'restructuring options', including finding a buyer to maximise the value of the business's assets (see the box on accelerated mergers and acquisitions and 'pre-packaged' administration, page 205).

Accurate, complete and up-to-date information and access to financial and legal advice from appropriately qualified professionals will significantly strengthen a director's position in the event of a court hearing. They would, for example, be vital in justifying a director's actions if faced with a claim for wrongful trading (see section 3).

A court will be reluctant to substitute its own commercial judgment for that of a director unless it considers that no reasonable director could have concluded the action taken was in the interests of the company. In cases where directors have taken the advice of properly qualified, competent professionals, judges are unlikely to claim they know better.

In some circumstances, there may be a conflict of interest between subsidiary and parent or between fellow subsidiaries, requiring separate legal and/or financial advice; for example, where it is proposed to use the assets of a doubtfully solvent subsidiary to secure the parent's indebtedness.

Directors may need to seek advice individually on how to minimise the personal risks involved in the management of a company that is approaching insolvency – see section 3.

Formulating a viable strategy

If the company's performance and prospects demand it, a board should formulate a strategy for restoring a company to a healthy financial position and avoiding formal insolvency proceedings. The action plan may involve one or a number of the following:

■ alternative trading strategies;

■ disposals;

■ maximising existing asset values;

■ cutting overheads;

■ delaying capital investment;

■ further bank finance (possibly with a grant of security);

■ converting debt to equity, converting short-term debt to long-term debt, or raising new equity;

■ an informal arrangement with major creditors or a voluntary arrangement;

■ arranging alternative sources of funding from other financiers, particularly where the bank is unlikely to advance further money.

The chosen strategy must have the support of the board (the full board if possible). In addition, its viability must be reviewed by appropriate advisers and its implementation constantly monitored.

At the very least, directors should review the strategy at each board meeting and have grounds for concluding that there is a reasonable prospect of avoiding insolvent liquidation.

They should reconsider the factors that underlay the development of the strategy and confirm whether in their view they are still valid, and that they are still reasonably achievable in a reasonable time, bearing in mind the company's cash requirements. A board might have committed the company to cutting overheads, delaying capital investment, relocating premises, selling part of the business or procuring fresh equity. At each meeting, the board will need to review whether the strategy is being implemented as envisaged and whether the underlying assumptions (for example, as to the value of properties) are still reasonable.

The valuations used should be realistic. The accounting principles upon which assets are valued for the purposes of the annual statutory accounts might not be appropriate. The realisable value of any asset will, of course, depend upon all the circumstances in which the asset is being sold. Discussions with a company's auditors or other financial adviser may be helpful on this point.

All decisions made and the reasons for them should be recorded in the minutes, as should any advice taken.

Holding regular meetings

Board meetings and other, more informal, meetings should be held at regular scheduled intervals, even daily. All directors should endeavour to be present in person or by phone/conference facility. Detailed minutes should be kept of all meetings and circulated promptly. Additional meetings should be called as and when new significant events occur. Briefing papers should be circulated before such meetings to promote informed discussion. Absent directors should be told as soon as possible of critical decisions taken at board meetings.

Involving all directors

Undoubtedly, the involvement of the finance director and any members of the management team responsible for credit control and assessing the current and future financial performance of a company will be key. Depending on the nature of a recovery strategy, input from sales, marketing and production executives may also assume a greater importance.

In most cases, however, it will be the non-executive directors who are best placed to assess whether a company is able to continue trading and, in particular, whether it can justify incurring fresh liabilities. Non-executives bring objectivity, experience and financial independence to the board. Where a company's prospects for survival are uncertain, their involvement will ensure that the interests of creditors and shareholders are not overlooked and will facilitate discussions with banks and other lenders.

Keeping major creditors informed

It's important that the distribution of information to creditors' groups is handled in an orderly way. Information to be released to creditors should be discussed with and, in some circumstances, presented by, the company's advisers. Where a strategy to be implemented requires creditors' support (principally that of the lending banks), a careful and clear presentation is required.

If a company's shares are publicly traded, directors will have to consider rules surrounding the release of price-sensitive inside information (see Chapter 5, particularly the case notes on pages 96 to 99).

Making announcements

The FSA's Disclosure and Transparency Rules oblige directors to make certain announcements to avoid the creation of a false market in the company's shares. Similar rules apply in the case of AIM companies. Bad news, in other words, cannot be kept hidden.

Announcing that a dividend might not be paid on a listed preference share, or that a company is in discussion with its bankers, will obviously have a marked effect on creditor confidence, and directors will need to consult their advisers about the timing of announcements.

They must, however, never lose sight of the fact that they can be guilty of a criminal offence if they:

- make any statement, promise or forecast they know to be materially misleading, false or deceptive;

- recklessly make (dishonestly or otherwise) any statement, promise or forecast that is materially misleading, false or deceptive;

- dishonestly conceal any material facts.

In each of these cases, directors will be guilty if they deliberately induced another person to deal in securities in a company on the basis of false information – or they were careless about what they said and its effect on investor behaviour. (See further at Chapter 5.)

Accelerated M&A and 'Pre-packaged' Administration

Currently, where a company is in financial trouble and its bankers and stakeholders are not prepared to fund for the long term, the directors will often be advised to consider an accelerated M&A strategy as the best means to achieve a better realisation for the creditors. This involves the fast-track marketing of the business by accountants and corporate advisers. Data rooms are set up for due diligence, and the M&A process (which would normally take months) is truncated to weeks or, in some cases, days.

Often, the outcome is that a buyer is found for the business but not one prepared to take the company with all its liabilities. The buyer therefore negotiates to acquire the assets of the business, leaving the rest behind. Once that deal is agreed, the company is put into administration. An insolvency practitioner is appointed, who then completes the sale (often helped by their previous involvement in the negotiations).

> These transactions, known as 'pre-packaged' administrations, will usually achieve a better result for creditors, and better protection for directors. They should only be entered into, however, with the benefit of professional legal advice.

3. Personal liabilities

Wrongful trading

In cases of insolvent liquidation, a director or shadow director (see question and answer box, page 208) can be required to contribute towards the debts or liabilities of a company. This provision does not merely apply to 'trading' activity: any act, or failure to act, that either increases or does not minimise losses to creditors can lead to liability.

The level of personal contribution will be determined by the court; it will reflect the extent to which the company's assets have been depleted by the director's conduct.

A court may make a contribution order if a liquidator can show that before winding-up began the person knew or ought to have concluded that there was no reasonable prospect of the company avoiding insolvent liquidation. The only defence open to a director in these circumstances will be that they took every step they could to minimise the potential loss to a company's creditors. The onus will be on the director to prove this defence.

The other main points about wrongful trading litigation are covered in the question and answer box opposite.

Disqualification

The Company Directors Disqualification Act 1986 (CDDA) provides that a director can be disqualified for a minimum period of two years for:

■ general misconduct in connection with companies;

■ conviction for an indictable offence in connection with the promotion, formation, management or liquidation of a company;

■ fraud in winding-up proceedings;

■ persistent breaches of companies legislation. (An example would be persistent default in filing any return, account or other document with the Registrar of Companies);

■ unfit conduct as the director of a company that has at any time become insolvent (ie gone into liquidation, administration or receivership).

The object of disqualification is twofold: to mark the court's disapproval and to protect the public. The corollary is that a director can attempt to show that their continued ability to act as a director would carry no risks to the public.

Sometimes, people are allowed to continue to act as directors subject to certain safeguards. There could, for example, be conditions that:

■ no cheque or financial agreement on behalf of a company is signed or executed by the director alone;

■ any loan owed by a company to the director is not repaid unless all creditors of the company are paid first;

■ the director shall not grant or accept any security over a company's assets.

Wrongful Trading Cases: Frequently Asked Questions

What if I resigned from the company. Will I still be liable?

Resigning will not, by itself, remove liability. In some circumstances, directors will be liable for all debts incurred up to their resignation.

Directors who resigned knowing insolvent liquidation was inevitable will, in principle, only be 'safe' if they can show they acted on that knowledge – ie took steps to protect their interests and those of creditors. They must have tried to persuade the other directors to follow what they believed to be the right course, perhaps using the threat of resignation as a negotiating tool. They must have expressed their views at a board meeting, preferably after producing a reasoned paper for the board, and made sure the minutes accurately recorded their views. In other words, the resignation must be capable of being seen as a response to a refusal to listen – the last resort of a responsible director.

A director who resigns in an attempt to avoid any future liability but continues to be involved with the management of the company as a shadow or de facto director may still be liable.

What standards will I be judged by?

In the first instance, a director is judged by the standards of the 'reasonable' director. This means they will be deemed to have the general knowledge, skill and experience that can be reasonably expected of a person carrying out the functions of a director. The mere fact that their own knowledge, skill and experience were inadequate for their role cannot be relied on as a defence. On top of that basic standard, a director will also be judged against the general knowledge, skills and experience they in fact possess. Judgments about the extent of these standards will be made case by case, taking into account both objective and subjective criteria. Directors with professional qualifications (eg accountants) may find that their professional body takes disciplinary action or at least seeks explanations of a director's conduct, particularly in relation to the signing off of previous years' accounts and the concept of a 'going concern'.

How are shadow directors defined?

A brief description of shadow directors and their legal position can be found on page 11.

The key point is that they can be liable for wrongful trading and be ordered to contribute to the assets of an insolvent company. A holding or parent company (and a director of such an entity) can be classed as a shadow director in certain circumstances; so can private equity houses and banks.

Liability arises when the shadow director's influence extends to the whole board. For example, a dominant investor can be a shadow director if the whole board, and not just the investor's representative on the board, was acting on its directions.

Are non-executives liable?

As their involvement may be critical when a company runs into difficulties, non-executive directors may find that they are as much at risk under the wrongful trading provisions as executive directors. This will depend on the circumstances of each case, but getting good advice early is key.

What will the court do?

Once liability is established, the court can order a director to 'make such contribution (if any) to the company's assets as it thinks proper'. It has complete discretion over the amount. In each case, it is likely to assess the difference between the actual net deficiency to creditors and what it would have been on the date when liquidation first appeared inevitable.

The court should also take account of the level of culpability of a particular director and recognise that other factors may have caused the deterioration in the net deficiency.

If it makes a declaration under the wrongful trading provisions, the court may also make an order to disqualify the director from being in any way concerned in the management of a company for a minimum period of two years (see page 206).

What can I do to protect myself?

The answer is found in section 2. In summary, it is to act responsibly and with integrity. Take an active role in monitoring the company's financial performance and never be afraid to raise concerns about solvency. Make sure what you say, and what you are told in response, are recorded. If fellow directors refuse to accept that the company is wrongfully trading, take no part in incurring further indebtedness.

Insist that any advice you and the board take is noted. It may be vital in disproving allegations by a liquidator and show that you and your fellow directors had reasonable grounds to believe insolvency could be avoided.

'Phoenix' syndrome

Legislation stipulates that the directors of an insolvent company must not, without leave of the court or approval of creditors, be directly or indirectly concerned in the promotion, formation or management of another company with a similar name within five years of the date of liquidation. These provisions relate to a name or trading name used by the liquidated company at any time in the 12 months before the liquidation.

If the business is acquired from an insolvency practitioner it can trade under a similar name provided a notice is sent to creditors making clear who from the old company is involved and what they are doing in the phoenix company. This notice must be circulated before a director of the insolvent company has any involvement with its 'namesake', but it does not provide a guarantee that the director will escape personal liability for the debts of the phoenix company. In many cases, a director in this situation should be advised to seek leave of the court before becoming directly or indirectly concerned with the 'new' company.

Misfeasance

Under the Insolvency Act, office holders and people involved in the promotion, formation or management of a company can be sued for misfeasance – the misapplication or retention of the company's assets or a breach of a fiduciary or other duty.

Misfeasance actions are brought in the name of the company. This distinguishes them from claims made under the provisions for wrongful trading, transactions at an undervalue and preferences – all of which are brought by a liquidator in their own right.

They are often seen as a simpler and, therefore, speedier means of bringing delinquent directors to book and of assessing compensation and damages.

Fraudulent trading

If any company carries on business with the intent to defraud creditors or for any other fraudulent purpose, a liquidator of the company can apply to a court for a contribution order against any person who was knowingly a party to the offence. Since they require fraudulent conduct – ie a deliberate intention to act to the detriment of another party – these types of claim are rare. Nonetheless, they remain a risk for directors who allow a company to continue to trade and incur liabilities when they know there is no real prospect that these will be paid.

Pensions

The Pensions Act 2004 includes provisions that could make a director personally liable for a pension scheme deficit (see Part 3 of Chapter 8). The so-called 'moral hazard' provisions allow the pensions regulator to serve contribution notices on certain third parties in addition to the company itself. These notices can impose liability for all or part of an occupational pension scheme's deficit and can be served on people (eg directors) who have attempted or been involved in an attempt to:

■ prevent the recovery of the whole or any part of a debt that was due, or might become due, from the employer in relation to the pension scheme;

■ prevent such a debt becoming due or compromise or reduce it (unless they acted in good faith).

While the pension fund itself is an unsecured creditor of a company, any deficit is likely to be large: it should never be ignored. Directors must also be aware of the possibility of conflict of interest where they sit on the trustee board and the board of the company.

Personal guarantees

Generally, directors are not personally liable for company debts. If, however, they have given personal guarantees on company loans, personal liability will be incurred. In some cases, bankruptcy orders may even result.

4. Other considerations

Transactions at an undervalue

A transaction will be regarded as being at an undervalue if the company does not receive any consideration for it – or the value of what it receives is significantly less than the value of what it provides. Examples of transactions at an undervalue include:

■ making a gift;

■ selling an asset for a price significantly less than its value;

■ guaranteeing a debt due from another group company.

A court can set aside a transaction at an undervalue and rule that a director has to help 'make good' the difference in value if:

■ the company is in liquidation or administration;

■ the transaction was made within two years before the start of the liquidation or administration;

■ the company was unable to pay its debts at the time of the transaction or became unable to pay its debts as a consequence of the transaction; and

■ the liquidator or administrator has made an application to the court for an order.

If the transaction is with a 'connected person', there is no need to prove that the company was unable or became unable to pay its debts. Connected persons are broadly defined: they include directors and shadow directors and their 'associates' (employers, close relatives, partners, companies controlled by them or their associates) and the associates of a company (other group companies).

A defence will be available if a court is satisfied that a company entered into a transaction in good faith and for the purpose of carrying on its business and there were reasonable grounds for believing that the transaction would benefit the company.

This defence protects a wide range of bona fide business transactions that might otherwise be vulnerable.

Preferences

A 'preference' occurs when a company does anything, or allows anything to be done, that puts one of its creditors, sureties or guarantors in a better position. Examples of preferences include:

■ payment of one creditor in full or in part when others remain unpaid;

■ granting security in respect of existing debts;

■ agreeing to pay a sum for services significantly more than their value;

■ making gratuitous payments to employees.

A preference can only be set aside if:

■ the company is in liquidation or administration;

■ the preference was made within six months before liquidation or administration – or two years in the case of transactions with 'connected persons' (see above);

■ the company was unable to pay its debts at the time it made the preference or became unable to do so as a result of the preference; and

■ the liquidator or administrator has made an application to the court for an order.

A transaction will only be deemed to be a preference (and therefore be capable of being set aside) if a company was 'influenced by a desire' to put a creditor or guarantor in a better position. It's not enough for a liquidator or administrator to show that a company was aware that the transaction would put a creditor in a better position – a positive wish to achieve this end is needed. Thus, a transaction made for a proper commercial reason is unlikely to fall within this provision.

A liquidator or administrator will generally look very carefully at transactions that benefit directors or their associates, either directly (eg paying directors' salaries or repaying directors' loan accounts) or indirectly (eg paying off an overdraft guaranteed by a director). Any requests by banks to secure current loans would therefore need to be examined carefully.

If the transaction is with a connected person, a company is presumed to have been influenced by a desire to put the creditor in a better position.

Void floating charges

A floating charge over the company's assets may be invalid if all of the following apply:

■ the company has gone into liquidation or administration;

■ the charge was created within 12 months before the start of the liquidation or administration – or two years if made in favour of a connected person;

■ the company was unable to pay its debts at the time the charge was created or became unable to do so as a consequence of the charge.

If the charge is created in favour of a connected person, there is no need for a liquidator or administrator to prove that a company was or became unable to pay its debts at the time or as a result of the transaction.

A floating charge will not be regarded as invalid if fresh consideration was provided for the security. 'Fresh consideration' includes: money paid, or goods or services supplied to a company; the discharge of any of a company's debts; interest payable under an agreement for the payment of money, supply of goods or services or discharge of debts.

It should be noted that under the provisions for transactions at an undervalue, preferences and floating charges, a company is deemed unable to pay its debts if it is proved that the value of its assets is less than the amount of its liabilities, taking into account its contingent and prospective liabilities.

Unlawful distributions

Assets may be passed to a company's members only if there are distributable profits (ie accumulated realised profits less accumulated realised losses) available for this purpose. If there are insufficient distributable reserves, a transaction with or payment to a shareholder could constitute an unlawful distribution of capital.

Directors of insolvent companies may breach their duties to creditors by making gratuitous distributions of assets. Such breaches cannot be waived by the shareholders.

These principles may also apply to distributions to persons connected with shareholders, such as other group companies.

5. Insolvency procedures

The following is a brief summary of insolvency procedures.

Administration

Administration will have one of three purposes. These, in order of desirability, are:

■ to rescue the company as a going concern – as opposed to selling its business and leaving a 'shell';

■ to achieve a better result for the creditors as a whole than if the company were wound up;

■ to sell the business or its assets in order to pay secured and/or preferential creditors (eg employees owed wages/holiday pay).

Administrators can only opt for the second purpose if they think that the first is not likely to be achieved or is not in the best interests of the creditors as a whole. They may not seek to achieve the third (fallback) purpose unless they think neither the primary nor the secondary purpose is likely to be achieved and no unnecessary harm will be caused to the interests of creditors as a whole.

The advantages of an administration order are that, without the consent of the administrator or the leave of the court:

■ a company cannot be wound up;

■ no legal proceedings can be taken against a company;

■ a receiver cannot be appointed and no other steps can be taken to enforce any security.

Once an administrator has been appointed they will take over the management of a company. This will relieve the directors of the critical day-to-day decisions and therefore minimise any risks of liability from that point on.

There are now three methods of appointing an administrator. These are explained below.

(i) Appointment by the court

A company, its directors or one or more creditors can apply to the court for the appointment of an administrator. The court may appoint an administrator only if it is satisfied that a company is, or is likely to become, unable to pay its debts and that the administration order is reasonably likely to achieve one of the three potential purposes explained above.

(ii) Appointment by the holder of a qualifying floating charge (QFC)

A QFC is a floating charge over the whole or most of a company's property and is created by a document that states that paragraph 14 of Schedule B1 to the Insolvency Act 1986 applies – or, more specifically, that the holder of the floating charge may appoint an administrator or (if the floating charge was created before 15 September 2003) an administrative receiver.

(iii) Appointment by the company or its directors

A company or its directors can appoint an administrator without a court order – ie make an 'out of court' appointment. They will, however, be unable to do so if within the previous 12 months any of the following applied:

■ the company was in administration but that administration came to an end at the behest of the company or its directors;

■ a voluntary arrangement ended prematurely;

■ a moratorium (obtained under schedule A1 of the Insolvency Act 1986) ended without a voluntary arrangement being approved.

Company Voluntary Arrangements (CVAs)

A CVA is an arrangement whereby the company continues to trade having reached an agreement with its creditors in satisfaction of its pre-existing debts, usually for a percentage of their face value. It can be used in cases where a liquidator or an administrator has already been appointed. The directors propose the arrangement and put it before unsecured creditors for approval. Copies of the agreed arrangement are then filed at court.

The procedure to put a CVA in place, and the implementation of a CVA, must be supervised by an accountant qualified to act in insolvency matters – ie an insolvency practitioner.

A CVA is not necessarily a 'once and for all' solution. A creditor may subsequently apply to a court on the grounds that there is significant irregularity with the CVA or that their interests are being prejudiced.

Until a CVA takes effect, a company will be unable to prevent creditors from enforcing their rights unless additional protection is sought from the court.

Voluntary winding-up

There are two types of voluntary winding-up. Both have the same result: bringing the life of a company to an end.

■ A members' voluntary winding-up depends on a declaration of solvency by directors. The directors swear that they have made a full inquiry into the company's affairs and have concluded that it will be able to pay all its debts, together with interest, within 12 months of the declaration. The company, at a general meeting, then passes a special resolution to wind the company up and appoints an insolvency practitioner as liquidator.

■ A creditors' voluntary winding-up is begun by the shareholders, who pass a resolution saying that the company cannot by reason of its liabilities continue its business and that it is advisable to wind it up. Subsequently, the creditors' wishes regarding the appointment of the liquidator and the conduct of the winding-up generally override the shareholders' wishes.

Compulsory winding-up

A compulsory winding-up can be started without the involvement of a company's shareholders. A petition is filed at court, and at a hearing some weeks later the court decides whether to make a winding-up order. If it does, the company is then in liquidation. The petition is usually filed by creditors.

Receivership

A receiver may be appointed by the holder of a fixed or floating charge granted by a company. Typically, a company will be served with a demand for repayment of monies due, and this will be followed by an appointment just hours later. Alternatively, a company may invite a charge-holder to appoint a receiver.

The receiver's task is to recover sums due to the secured lender or to realise the lender's security.

Historically, an administrative receiver has been appointed by the holder of a floating charge covering the whole, or substantially the whole, of the company's property. Receivers, by contrast, have been responsible solely for assets subject to a fixed charge.

Administrative receivership, however, is dying out: the provisions of the Enterprise Act 2002 effectively abolished it for charges created after 15 September 2003.

Your professional development starts here

Why learn?

No matter how experienced you are you can never be too highly qualified to ignore the need to continually enhance your expertise.

The IoD offers a series of development services to address a whole range of needs at senior level:

- Business orientated courses and conferences
- The Certificate and Diploma in Company Direction
- Chartered Director
- Bespoke consultancy services
- In-company development
- Executive coaching

The IoD focuses on senior level professional development in both the public and private sector. Contact us today to find out how we can help you and your organisation.

T: +44 (0)20 7766 2601
E: professionaldev@iod.com
W: www.iod.com/development

Index